Copyright © 2024 By Pamela Matilda

All rights reserved. No part of this book may be reproduced or transmitted in any form or by any means without written permission from the author.

Disclaimer:

This book is an autobiography.
Names have been changed to protect both others and myself.

How to grow sunflowers

an autobiography

By

Pamela Matilda

For my son, who continues to inspire me. A life saver, my reason for being, my angel ...

Contents

1. This is me! (Introduction)
1. The beginning!
2. Leaving home/nurse training partying days, including mum and dads break up
3. Ass A, The Heart Breaker (Albert)
4. The Destroyer (Matthew)
5. The disclosure and the running events (Jerry)
6. The end of the road and coming back
7. Borderline Personality Disorder; who the hell am I?
8. Hold on, There's more!
9. Here I am! Hopes & Dreams

1. This is me! Introduction

This is my story. The story of my life. Why and how I came to be the Empowered woman I am today.

The trials and tribulations I suffered, from a difficult childhood, to suffering domestic violence, coping with single parenthood, coming to terms with my mental health condition and my endless search for acceptance. The losses and knock backs I have struggled through. When it all became too much. How my spiritualism helped me. The battle I have constantly fought to stay well, and keep on going, no matter what. Throughout that path, trying to reach my goals and aspirations, trying to be me! Most of all, trying to find my dream come true, my happy ever after, finding my inner peace, finding, and learning to love the real me!

Why am I writing it? Well, who knows?! Partly for therapy for myself, to piece together the jumble of thoughts and memories and somehow make sense of it all. Hopefully heal internal wounds and scars I have, reach acceptance, maybe I will feel I have achieved something, maybe this will help people to understand dv and having a mental health condition, and maybe, most importantly I will inspire someone and help just one person through their difficult times? Maybe ……..

I commenced writing my story after having received some counseling; I was recommended to write my feelings down in a journal, little did I know when I started this journal, it would end up turning into a book!
I have been attempting to do this book for 8 years (since 2015) and I never get round to completing it. Why couldn't I?
 Fear of finding about me, myself, who I am, maybe I won't like me?!

Fear of people laughing at me, fear of hurting those I love. But I must do it and I shall! It is now February 2023 and my aim is to complete it by the end of the year.

This story is not written with malice, or regrets. Not intended with a means to pass blame, upset or cause trouble for anyone. Words may hurt but not intentionally so, it's just the truth, my truth, my story, and I am TRULY sorry if this book does hurt some people.

(For confidentiality, to protect myself and others, I have changed names. This is also why I have used a different name as author.)

I would like to name two people to give a big thank u and a hug.

My son. You have been my Carer, you have saved my life on many occasions. You have had to live through and suffer from my bad decisions and bouts of ill health.

I know because of all that, you lost some of your childhood and that is something that no amount of therapy will take away the guilt and sorrow I feel inside of me. But yet, throughout all the hard times, you have kept on going. You continued in your life, with a few glitches, still picking yourself up, dusting yourself down, and carrying on! And you continue to aspire and aim to reach your goals and aspirations. You are no longer a boy; you are a man, and you are so beautiful. You are my love, my life, my everything. My heart continues to beat because of you. Thank you, I love you.
xxx

M, you know who you are, you motivated me, you picked me up and challenged me on my bad days and gave me the kick up the backside I needed to do this, it's been a while since I last saw you, but it means a lot, so much. You will always have a space in my heart. And, of course, not forgetting my mum adored you when she was our dinner lady at school, she always said you had the most beautiful blue eyes! Thank you. x

I hope reading this book gives you what it needs to give.

Blessed Be xxx

2.

The Beginning
Every Day

May everyday

the sunshine

the flowers blossom

and the colours just brighten your day!

May everyday

Mother Earth shine

down on you

and guide you on your way!

Well, I was born in 1969 when it was the era of the hippie, free love and the first man landed on the moon.

Mum wanted to call me Lunar and my goodness how glad am I she didn't do it.

There was also my sister, who is two years older than me.

Mum and Dad struggled at the beginning. It was hard, they would row because of the stress but nothing any married couple doesn't do, is it?

My memories as a child are a fuzzy blur, for some reason, a lot of it I have either blocked out or just have no memory of, I don't know why. It is particularly hard for me of late as a few people from school have contacted me on Facebook and although I recall some of their names, I often have no memory of them and me. I recall some happy times, special occasions, family gatherings and trips out. Several memories fill me with sadness, a lot of them being of my parents, of their love/hate and volatile relationship.

My sister and I recall night times, when a lot of the time, we would lay in our beds with our pillows over our heads to try and muffle out the sound of raised voices, fighting and hearing our mum sobbing in sadness and desperation.

Mum was 4 ft 11, she was chunky but cute, with dark hair cut in a pixie cut, flattering her chic beautiful face frame. Big brown/hazel eyes and a lovely smile that would light up her face.

I always had a lot of love for my dear mother, but a lot of my childhood and early puberty, I think I pushed her away a lot. I look a lot like her, plus we are both water star signs.

When she was happy, she was so lovely, she had little, chunky cheeks that would bulge slightly when she smiled. She was also fun to be around, liked a laugh and we really had some great times with her.

She could also be quite emotional and nervy; dad and their rows affected her. When rowing with my dad, her anger did scare me as it equally did when she became distressed. I felt she was out of control, little did I know that what she felt helpless and in love with a man, my dad, besotted with him, whom she knew she had no control over what he did. Who maybe also saw her life slipping from within her grasp. She also suffered with her Menstrual Cycle, suffered bad PMT, which would display itself with mood swings and depression. Dad often was the one who would bear the brunt of it.

Mum did have a temper; her side of the family were renowned for the 'venomous tongue' that they all appeared to have.Mum would hurl everything at you verbally, she would retain things people did wrong or hurt her about and throw it all out at you when she got upset with you.

Mum struggled a lot when we were growing up, she often would take her situation out on us, with her snapping or losing her temper. I do not blame her for this, not now I know why. It must have all been so hard for her.

Dad was tall and slender with short blonde hair, receding, and blue eyes. He had a moustache, the fashion, looked a bit like a famous actor, Shoestring. He was attractive and woman would often appraise him when we were out.

My dad, I saw as very much the parent in control, although sometimes too much; so much so, he came across business like and cold. He was a successful, professional man whom I thought always came out on top.

 However, he had a temper, which would bring out a cold and mean streak, mostly expressed at poor mum.

He was always charming to people outside of the family, my friends loved him, most people did, especially women. He was a terrible flirt, couldn't help himself.

I recall occasions where we would be at a social event, dad would be outrageously flirting with different women and mum would sit quietly with my sister and myself, holding her head down to save herself from seeing and the embarrassment.

Dad used to find me hard to deal with, I think. He worked a lot, it seemed a stressful job, he was always busy and tired. Coming home to hyper me seemed to agitate him quite a bit.

I think because I looked a lot like mum and similar in our ways, it may be made him resentful, sometimes, if he was having issues with her, he would be quite cruel and harsh towards me.

He also took pleasure in teasing me, sometimes taking it too far. However, on a good day, he was great fun to be around and I loved him.

He was heavily into fishing and watching football, so I would often take to going with him, so I could have quality dad/daughter time with him and we hadfun! I remember one time, I caught 3 trout, as we went to go to his local pub to have a drink and catch up with some friends, he told me not to tell people how many fish I caught as he hadn't caught any. To his embarrassment, I didn't do that, instead telling everyone! I still go on about it to this day and we do laugh.

I don't blame mum and dad for the difficult times of my childhood, they both played a part in it, but through their own issues that they were having. I loved them both and still do. They made their mistakes but also gave me so much love and some happy memories.

My sister, Amy and I had a tumultuous relationship, love, and hate. There was always sibling rivalry with her having the need to compete with me.

She had the gift of captivating other's attention, she had a face like a porcelain doll, a chic shaped face with blonde bobbed hair. Huge grey/blue eyes that sparkled, opaque like skin that glistened. She was so beautiful and innocent looking.

Whilst I only captured attention of others in the only way I was able to, by being naughty.

I was considered a 'problem child'. I was tall, skinny, lanky legs, very tomboyish looking, with big blue eyes and wild blonde hair and a protruding chin which I hated, I looked like a pixie! I was quite hyperactive, could not sit still, very restless at time, which my parents found difficult.

I was socially awkward, found it hard to make friends, preferring instead to play alone, imaginary play, with imaginary friends.

My sister and I competed a lot, mainly I feel, due to how mum and dad treated us. During times when they were not getting on, they argued quite a lot and during these times, they didn't have much time for us. So, we competed for that time.

I was often referred to as the problem child, how I was a difficult baby and how perfect my sister was. There were sometimes jokes by my sister of the beauty and the beast, you can guess which one I was! I must admit, I did feel jealous, longing for acceptance for my wild ways, craving love and attention. Sometimes, negative attention was better than no attention at all, so I would play up, self-destruct.

There were, however, occasions the tables turned when, on the rare occasion, I did good and was praised for it.

When I was receiving that attention, Amy would somehow manage to turn it around to her, often by teasing, provoking, hurting me, of course when no-one was looking. This would continue until sadly; I could cope no longer, and I would retaliate. She had the gift of drama, a great actress and this would result in me being chastised and punished.

Despite the difficulties, my childhood was not all bad.

We had some great holidays as a family to Scotland, Cornwall, Norfolk etc. Weekends, we would often go out, seaside trips, long walks with our dog Sindy, picnics, etc.

Dad was a career man, ambitious and driven. He encouraged me to aim high, to achieve, his hard-working ethic instilled in me a desire to be like him professionally.

Mum was a real home maker, she cooked and cleaned to perfection, taking pride how our home looked.

Our home always smelt lovely, with aromas of the beautiful food mum was cooking. She made everything herself, baked to perfection, my favorite being her Millionaire's Shortbread and Peppermint slices. She devoted her time being a wife and mum, she was amazing now I think back, I did love her so.

I feel now, maybe mum wanted the 'perfect home and family', for it to be so amazing, that she did such a fantastic job, dad would not want to leave. I am not sure, to this day, she enjoyed the role she made for herself, it often seemed an obsession, she would be tense and on edge.

I recall we lived in a village outside Bedford for a while, when I was very young, before I started school.
We had a lovely neighbour who used to make me fresh milkshakes and the most amazing tuna macaroni, yummy, I still make that today.

I had a pretend friend at this point, whom I loved dearly, his name was Don and he went everywhere with me. I think he was a man, who protected me and made me laugh. Mum would laugh as she recalled when we used to go shopping and we'd go on the bus, it would be crowded and I would refuse to allow anyone to sit beside me, saying Don was sitting there!

I don't recall much else about living there apart from I think this was the time I got given a brown teddy which for some reason I used as a protector, I don't know why but teddy helped me when something awful happened to me as a child. This came out when I had trauma therapy and was under hypnotherapy, but this memory is still a blank today and something I may have to face later in life.

Just before I was due to start school, Dad got a promotion and we moved to a lovely village just outside of Bury St Edmund's.

Sometime before this move, I suffered a tragic loss. Dad was driving and said he thought he saw Don and then the car braked screeched and Dad told me he had run over him and he had gone, I was devastated as at this time, he was all I felt I had.

When we moved to Bury, I must have been 4yrs old, I was so determined to make new friends that on the day we moved, I was seen to be standing on front lawn of our new home, saying 'hello I just moved here' to everyone who walked past. Bless!

I had an unsettled childhood, suffering strange mood swings, often hearing voices and having a lust for imaginary play, spending hours escaping into Barbie land or shutting myself into my room and reading my Enid Blyton books, imagining being a part of the Famous Five gang and their adventures.

I also had a China canary that I thought was real, devoting endless hours feeding and watering him, chatting away to him. My best escape were our family dogs, Sindy and Candy.

Sindy was a beautiful cavalier, tri coloured; black and white with brown patches and the hugest eyelashes that she would flutter at you to get what she wanted.
She was the soppiest animal you could meet, so much so, when we had an electrician let himself into our home to do some work, she was the perfect guard dog, jumping up at him and licking him in a very welcoming manner!   Sindy gave endless, uncomplicated love, never pushed me away and never shouted. I would spend hours with her,
talking, telling her my deepest secrets and feelings, knowing it would go nowhere.

I loved Candy also, but she joined the family later on, as a puppy, and

Sindy was getting on a bit.

Candy was a Cocker Spaniel with huge brown eyes and a sad face. She had Candy coloured shiny fur, so silky to touch. She was sensitive and a little clingy, always wanting our undivided attention.

At first, they got on but once Candy grew up, she wanted to be the alpha in the pack and started to attack Sindy, poor old Sindy was too old and weak to defend herself and would howl as Candy gripped her teeth around her neck. I would be terrified, screaming and crying, my heart racing. Candy would continue gripping hard, snarling loudly as he lips salivated in excitement. Dad would slowly take his time, strolling over and separating them. I still don't know why he took his time, especially when we would be getting so distraught. I think they were my first panic attacks I suffered in life. I recall not being able to breathe and just screaming in fear.

In the end, poor Sindy developed health problems, kidney failure so mum and dad did the right thing, taking her to the vets and having her put down. We did a special funeral for her in the garden, burying her with her blanket and special toys.

My childhood was erratic, filled with moments both of happiness and sadness. Often influenced by mum and dad's relationship. I cannot say who was to blame for their many arguments, I would see both behaving in ways I did not like.

However, I do feel dad's flirting and infidelities, which were obvious to see, massively affected it, as well as taking a toll on mum's mental state of health.

They both had tempers, mum would sometimes lash out at me when I made her angry. Dad, believed in corporal punishment so would smack my bottom or hand it I was naughty.

With dad, mum appeared quite scared of him, but when she went, she went, and nothing would stop her. She kept things inside of her, I think because she had given up on trying to talk to him about how she felt, so it would all build up. Then when he triggered her temper, it would all come out. Dad was a result of his stressful work life, lived on the edge, a stress head, and a hot head.

The tension and stress was always in the air, they were both like ticking time bombs.

I recall one situation that deeply disturbed me. Dad was unwell with a chest infection. Dad took to the sofa, blanket and hot water bottle, hurling demands at mum and being very grumpy. It was a blustery day, heavy rain and high winds. Dad demanded mum walk to the shop and get him some Lucozade. It looked like a storm was building outside, so mum explained she would rather not go outside with the weather as it was. He kept demanding and mum put her foot down, refusing. Within a split second, dad was standing up in front of poor mum. He took hold of her and proceeded to pull and drag her out of the house, locking the door behind him. Hearing mum outside, crying pitifully, I felt helpless, too scared to help her.

Poor mum was so insecure and emotionally fragile, looking back, it is no surprise really and I definitely do not blame her for how she was when I was a child.

My dad's temper was hard to be around, and his infidelities bore her down.

When they argued about it, he would always say she was crazy, that it was all in her head, but I remember things he used to do, his behaviour around other women.

Such as I recall having a babysitter, a lady dad knew from work and on a couple of occasions, my sister and I recall coming into the lounge and catching her draped on my dad, sitting on his lap; she would soon jump off when we disturbed them.

My parents struggled to cope with me. I don't know why but I just couldn't help myself being destructive in my manner and ways, I guess at the time, bad attention was better than no attention as my sister seemed to get so much love and attention and they seemed so proud of her.
I didn't feel I fully fitted in and I always struggled to, causing myself to feeling rejected and alone .

It was like I had a self-destruct mechanism, the more I tried to behave, the more I messed up and disappointed my parents.
I spent a lot of my time at home in my bedroom, alone, after being told off.
I'd escape in my imaginary world again. I recall reading the secret garden and I loved it, this special hidden garden, a secret, for my eyes only. I loved it so I would take to going in my garden pretending to be the little girl discovering the secret garden for the first time, smelling the beautiful flowers in bloom, hearing the birds sing and the sun beaming down warming my body, it was fantastic!

When I look back and think 'Who did I really love?' well, I loved different people in different ways. For example, I always sought and delighted in dad's approval and praise of me but I would seek

mum out for a hug and reassurance when I was upset.

I remember a deep love for my grandparents on both sides. I felt I was loved unconditionally by them, for them, I was not a disappointment. As mum and dad's rows got worse, I found myself spending more time at both grandparents, which was not a bad thing at all. I had some fun times at their homes, I felt at peace, I was allowed to be a child and there were no expectations on me.

Granddad L was a large, tall man with big blue eyes (where I get mine from) He was like a gentle giant, 6ft 3, with a big cuddly belly. He was my teddy bear who gave the best bear hugs. London born and bred, he was born of Irish Gypsy blood, with a broad Cockney accent and a cheeky boy glint in his eye. He had a wicked sense of humour, was always making me laugh and smile.

His dad had been a rag and bone man, working-class and very hard working. Grandad would recall, as a child, money was tight. The bakers horse and cart would come once a week, the smell of delicious warm, fresh baked rolls would make his lips salivate. Having a fresh bread roll in those days was a delicacy. How, every so often, his friends and he would be waiting. One would stand talking to the baker and the others would steal hot rolls and run down the road, the rolls would be so hot, they had to keep throwing and catching them, he would chuckle to himself as he told me.

Grandad was brought up tough, was taught to be hard, to be able to defend himself. He was a quiet, placcid man. Huge devotion to his family, and so protective of us all. He could do magic tricks with playing cards, I recall sitting there watching him repeatedly showing me the same tricks every time I visited,

I did not get bored as he was amazing. Oh, how I loved him!

I took after my Nan L a lot, having several of her attributes, scatty, funny, a lot of love to give.

A short, stout lady with immaculately permed hair, a beautiful smile that lit up her face, kind eyes and a cheekiness about her. She loved her gold jewellery, would always be seen with gold chains and pendants, rings, and bracelets, smelling of Estee Lauder 'Youth Dew' perfume.

She took pride in her appearance. She was a Witch (how people were referred to at the time), I think as I recall her having friends over, she would take them into the kitchen and would read their palms or tea leaves, I was not meant to go in there, but I often stood outside behind the kitchen door listening.

It fascinated me, but if I asked her about it, she would tell me it was old women's stuff and not something I needed to know about.

It saddens me now recalling this, as I wish I had asked more as I got older. I do not think I did because she acted like it was a closed subject and for some reason, did not wish for me to know about it.

I am now however, also Wiccan, as is my son. Huge regrets I did not push for information from her when she was alive. I think I just respected her wishes for me not to know; I realise now it was her way of protecting me.

Her living her life as she did; an eccentric, wacky and quite obviously spiritual woman, I do not think she was not taken seriously by many, in those days, witchcraft was frowned upon.

I recall she did not have many friends, only people of her own kind who understood her gifts and beliefs.

Although we were never told much about her heritage, I know her dad was a boxer. With that and the palm and tea-leaf reading, I wonder if she was of Gypsy descent.

For myself, I know some may scorn at my beliefs, but I refuse to hide them and am proud of my family, heritage and ancestors. I am making a conscious effort of being open about my gifts and beliefs, I am proud of who I am. I just wish my nan had been able to be the same, that makes me sad thinking about it.

As for Grandad T, I was his pride and joy, the apple in his eye. He was a short, petite man, with salt and pepper coloured hair that was styled in a flick at the front. He wore suits, fitted neatly to his body shape, with polished shoes. I was his little flower and he liked nothing more than combing my hair, which he did with so much love and tenderness.

He spent many hours with me as a child, going for long walks, watching boxing, playing sweet shop and cars. He embraced my weirdness, even enjoying listening to the music I liked, we both shared a love of Shaky and Aha and would often spend the afternoon listening to their music.

Grandma T was a woman not to be messed with. She was a stout, old fashioned lady. Grey set hair, formal attire was worn at all time, for her, appearance was everything. She wore thick set glasses that she would use to look down at people if she disapproved of them. She wasn't upfront with her love but showed it in her own way. She spoilt me with what she did; treating me to nice gifts, cooking for me, she was not very expressive apart from when she was disproving. She did, however, have a funny side.

Once, we all went out as a family into town, it had been snowing and my sister

and I were skidding and sliding down the path. Nan sternly asked her to stop and proceeded to say 'stop that! You will make it slippery and some silly old fool with fall…….' Just as she was finishing, she slowly slid to the floor, landing with a thud and an outburst of laughter from us all. Luckily, she saw the funny side and we were not punished.

Christmases were fun in some ways but not in others. All the grandparents would come and stay, I would be so happy but also on edge as my mum did not get on with nan (her mum in law) as nan did not approve of my mum and always made it obvious It would be a very tense time.

I recall nothing mum did was ever good enough and, in the end, I think she just gave up trying. Nan would make comments about mum, such as how mum had 'thick' legs, how her food was never cooked right etc.
 I remember how poor mum's face would drop forlornly, dad would say nothing, she was on her own.
Sometimes, she would answer her back sharply to defend herself, but she always ended up being the one in the wrong,
 resulting in mum and dad arguing with dad blaming her, saying she was causing trouble when there didn't need to be any.

It was difficult growing up around this. However, I always remember the excitement of going to bed at night, my sister and myself on the floor in her bedroom and nan snoring in her bed, mouth wide open, sometimes we would hold her nose in her sleep or stuff tissue in her mouth, it was so funny, us two snickering quietly, nearly wetting myself with laughter, not realising how dangerous it was, we were just children! Very happy childhood memories for me. Memories also of getting into bed with Grandad T in the morning for a cuddle and a story, of which he would make up as he went along, always with some weird funny ending.

I do have some really happy memories. BBQs in the summer, with Dad singeing all the food, but his amazing home-made ribs literally made my lips water. Family get togethers, both nan and grandads competing for our attention. Chalk and cheese was an understatement, one was rich and conservative, the others working-class Londoners, who would say it as it is. Chalk and cheese did not get on or mix well!

Back to my childhood. Every summer, we would take a long drive to Scotland and stay in this beautiful cottage, trout fishing on the lakes, long walks and exciting adventures...
It was a fun time, exploring the rocks and jagged cliffs and hills, seeing the beautiful countryside.
The smells were amazing, nothing like a sweet smell of sheep poo poos! And I always knew I was there when I'd wake up to the sound of lambs bleating.
Every holiday we had, there would always be some sort of row between mum and dad, but my sister and I would leave them to it and go off exploring.
Or I would take myself to my room and escape in my books, spending endless hours whatever the weather reading, falling into the characters in the book, being them, becoming them.

I think when you suffer a hard time, that can overshadow the good times in that same era. I remain positive, concentrating on the good, not the bad memories. I am grateful for my childhood.

Being a teenager was hard. I don't have much memory recollection of this time in my life and that hurts as I know there were some happy times.
Perhaps by writing this, I will recover some of these happy memories as I explore my inner mind and go back to that place.

I always found it hard finding friends, I was a wonderer, a day dreamer and I didn't seem to have the skills or confidence to hold a conversation,
and if so, keep the attention of whom I was talking to. Nowadays, people would call me socially awkward, maybe even Neuro-Diverse.
I was seen as a weirdo at school, the harder I tried to be accepted, the more of a mess I made, causing myself to be
 the laughingstock in our class.

It was then, when I was getting desperate and a not very popular girl, Tracey, befriended me.

Tracey had gone to the same primary school as me, was a strange girl and like me, not accepted. She was adopted and quite mixed up; I think.

At upper school she had not many friends in school but had friends with older boys who had left school and used to hang in town all the time. She took me under her wing and for the first time I felt wanted and I had a real friend! I was happy.
However, the more I got to know Tracey, the more I learnt that things were not as it seemed.
She shop lifted and started to train me to also, saying this is what people who want to be her friends must do. Even when my mum and dad took us both out for the day, whilst mum and dad were window shopping, Tracey and I would be

looking at what we could steal and make money from, of which I had to give to her.

I started to truant, and my studies suffered, I was at the time prepared to risk it, as far as I was concerned, having a friend and being happy was more important to me. And did I regret that decision later on!
Terry and I got close, and I started to meet this older mate of hers, skinheads who sold magazines, they seemed nice but I didn't realise atthe time what magazine they were selling (National Front magazine) and the pleasure they took out of beating up anyone not English.

One day, I was staying at Terrys' house, she said she was going to run me a bath, I thought how considerate it was. She told me to leave the door unlocked so she could come and talk to me. I got in the bath and started to relax. What happened next was awful and a complete betrayal

of our friendship and my trust for her.
As I was relaxing, I closed my eyes. It was then I heard Terry come in, she said keep relaxing, so I did. I felt unsettled as she could see me naked in the bath.
She said she will wash my back and started to lather up a flannel.
She did wash my back but as she did so, her hands proceeded to wander to other areas of my body and I froze, not knowing what to do as she continued to wash and touch all my body, breathing heavily. All of a sudden, as if I'd just woken up from a dream, I sat bolt upright and said 'stop, I don't want that'. She frowned and shrugged her shoulders, as she left the room saying 'what other friends do you have,' laughing to herself.

We never talked about that incident, but it was then, I started to back off; the truanting stopped as did the shop lifting. I started to make new friends who accepted me for me. I could not let them too close though, in case I got hurt again, so I learnt to keep people at bay.

I started to find out more about Terry and her 'older friends. They worked for National front and Terry idolised them, so much so, they shared her for sex, and she stole for them so they made money from her.

The icing on the cake was when one day, my dear friend who lived in my village, David, did not come to school, he was African, he was walking home after school the day before and a gang of young skinhead men stopped him, held him down whilst some of them attempted to colour him white with a chalk and beat him with a black board rubber, he ended up in hospital and not long after, the whole family moved away, I was told to London.

After this, I never spoke to Terry again and I developed a pure hatred for racism and intolerance of other cultures in our country, still do this day.

After school, I went to college, it was in another town. I had withdrawn into myself again and struggled to find friends. I recall many lunch times going and sitting in the college toilets to pass the time and to stop people thinking I am alone and without any friends, which I was. It was a lonely time. No matter how I tried I couldn't fit in, I'd either be out of control hyper or low and withdrawn, people couldn't cope with it, they found it weird.

I do not recall many happy memories of my college days really, there may have been some but it maybe I have forgotten them.

I often had problems on the school bus, there were often not places to sit apart from the back seat at the bottom floor with all the troublemaker boys. They enjoyed my shyness and I think they got a kick out of embarrassing me.

The jibes about my over developing breasts were constant, the redder my face got, the more they did it.

One day on the way to college, I yet again had no choice but to sit on the back seat, and as I went to sit down, one of the boys grabbed me by the hips and forced me down onto his lap.
I could not move, yet again I froze. They all jeered, saying I must be enjoying it else I would be frigid. The bus was bumpy, at each bump, he would proceed to grind me further down onto him, I could feel he was aroused. He then asked his mates if they would like some, one said 'let me feel those jugs!' the boy who had hold of me leant me towards his mate whilst still holding my hips and forcing me onto his erection.
His mate proceeded to grope my breasts, by this point I was crying, I remember lots of people watching, looking scared but no one helped me. At the end of the

journey, all of the boys on the back seat had had a fumble, I was passed along to each. I tolerated it and as soon as the bus stopped, I ran off the bus and into college to the safety of the toilets to get my head together.

When I got home, I told my parents a bit of what happened, but I couldn't everything, I was so ashamed I didn't stop it. I think dad called the college and the boys were spoken to, but basically, they got away with it.

Having this happen to me at a young age scarred me. I withdrew further into myself. I started not caring if people like me or not.

It was then, Martha on my college course, befriended me, she introduced me to the friends she had made, and college became more bearable.

I completed two years, one year there and the last year at another, where I had to resit my O'Levels and did pretty good, having enough grades to be able to apply for a career I had always wanted to do.
To be a nurse.

3.

Leaving home & The Break-up

Waiting.....

Waiting,

not knowing the purpose of life

unsure which way to go

undercurrents of confusion and torment

as the days go slowly by

Waiting,

Lost

After getting the grades I needed at college, I started to apply for Enrolled Nurse (MH) Training. We were allowed to put 3 choices in the application form, I put South Ockendon, Chelmsford and Ipswich.

Mum and dad were an amazing support. When I got the interviews, they came with me in the car, dropping me off so I did not have to stress about getting there. Luckily enough, I was offered all three hospitals, I chose to be closer to home so chose Ipswich.

I remember the day I moved to Ipswich, into the nurse's flat so I could start my nurse training. Mum and dad packed their car up with my stuff and bags full of produce mum had brought for me. The mood was odd, dad was buzzing and full of pride, but mum appeared subdued. It wasn't till weeks later that mum told me how hard it was letting me go and how she had cried all the way home in the car. They dropped me off and helped me unload the car of my things.

I had a nice welcome to my flat, my flatmates Penny and Amanda were great, they introduced themselves and then took me to a pub.

I settled in well, loving my nurse training and having lots of fun socialising, many doctor and nurse parties and lots of drinking!
To be honest, I started to drink very heavily, great way to cover pain I guess, so much so, I believe I may have still been under the influence when I sat my nurse exams, so goodness knows how I passed!

I lost my virginity at the nurses' flat to Matthew, my then boyfriend, it was all quite messy, seemed to be all about him, lots of pumping in and out of me, my insides dry and painful as he did so.
To be honest, I really couldn't see what all the fuss was about this sex malarky!
He ended it with me a while later, my way of coping was drinking, clubbing, parties, and men.

Somehow, I had got it into my head that to get a man, let him have you,

give him what he wants, I just do not know. All I do know was I had this huge need to be loved, so that was my conquest but also my vulnerability.
 It was only after having slept with several men, I realised how stupid I was being, that feeling of being dirty, a slut; not something I was proud of. I also got hurt, because of my behaviour, men saw me as an object to have sex with, I had no self-respect, and they had no respect for me. I developed an 'I don't give a shit' attitude to protect myself and help me save face from all the rejections. But deep down; I had a heart of gold, my vulnerable inner child just craving the feeling of being loved and accepted.

Even though I had made friends and was getting on well with my studies, I still felt low. There is a saying, 'you can be in a crowded room full of people, yet still feel alone. That was me. I would often just sit in my room, feeling lost and alone.

Sitting looking out of my window, watching the world go by, feeling melancholy, even a little home sick. It was then I started to write, jot down my feelings on paper, formulating them together into poetry or proses.

It was at this time I met Harry. He was a USAF Serviceman. Six foot 3, chunky, dark hair, big blue eyes, with a smile that melted many a woman. Drove a Honda Fire Blade motorbike and was basically drop dead gorgeous! We started seeing each other, I thought it was something, but I realised he did not feel the same when he had a motorbike accident, and I went to visit him in hospital.

I hadn't heard from him for some time, so I called his dorm. His friend answered and told me he was in hospital after having a motorbike accident. I felt sick inside, thinking of him in a ward, no family and no way to contact me. I checked visiting hours and soon headed to the hospital, excited at the thought of seeing him but trepidation over how injured he may be. He looked surprised to see me, but also appeared on edge, looking at the entrance every now and again. He managed to lean forward in his hospital bed to kiss me, gave me a hug, quickly saying he doesn't need visitors and how I should go home. I sat beside him, saying I care about him so will stay a while. He looked uncomfortable but I just dismissed it as maybe he was feeling drugged up or in pain. He had fractured his leg and it was in traction.

As we were talking, a young pretty, blonde-haired lady entered the bay, heading towards Harry. He looked nervous as she stood over him and put her arms around him, leaning forward and giving him a long loving kiss. She looked at me, then kissed him again, muttering 'who are you?'. Harry told her I am just a friend, that I shall be leaving now. I felt sick inside, plus also a deep rage building, I wanted to scream at him how he is a cheat, how he is using and hurting us both. But something stopped me, instead, I stood up, said 'nice to meet you, bye Harry,' I held my head high and walked out of the ward, past the nurses I knew, keeping my face stoic, walking through the hospital and to outside, where I found my car. Getting into the car, shutting myself in, lowering the visor and then; feeling safe and alone, I cried my eyes out, sobbing at the hurt and humiliation I was feeling. I got back to the flat and my dear friend Penny gave me the biggest hug, talking to me about liking myself, respecting myself and not letting men use me like they were doing.

I carried on my nurse training studies, spending some free time heading home to see mum and dad.

Whilst I was home, I started to notice my dad was looking preoccupied, as if he had other things on his mind, going out a lot 'to work', coming home in different hours. Mum was keeping herself busy, keeping our home immaculate, just how dad liked it and would demand it stay that way.

I had started to hang about with Cordelle and Violet, they were Matthew's sisters. Their mum and dad always welcomed me with open arms, spoiling me with love and making their home seem like a second home to me.

I felt welcome and loved, it was a happy place to be. I would stay out all hours, going there for a home cooked meal, sitting there watching the way they interacted together as a family, lots of laughs and banter. I remember sitting there, feeling a little jealous about how close they were and how happy they all seemed to be together, wishing my family was like that. Also, feeling humbled and happy to be part of this special time. We would

would spend many evenings in Cordelle's and Violette's room, music on, putting our make up on, dressing up in bright and glamorous outfits and prepping ourselves for our night out. Heading out to town, meeting other friends, starting in pubs, and ending up in a club, whether Reflex or Vienna. Dancing and drinking together, even doing the same moves to certain songs we all loved. Girl power all the way!

I did meet a couple of men, but nothing serious, a small case of harmless flirting and banter, liking myself enough to know I am worth more than just sleeping with. I was happy with that.

After I qualified, I got a job as Nurse Practitioner in a Community Resource Unit and moved into a house not far from work, with my work colleague Molly. It was a small, terraced house, very rustic with Molly's art scattily placed around the house, rustic, wicker furniture with different coloured throws and shawls draped over the sofas. A beautifully scatty and ecclectic home, with an air of calm filling it. Aromas of spices and herbs overflowing each room and Molly concocted the most deliciously mouth-watering vegetarian dishes. I was happy here.

After what I think was two years, we went our separate ways, I got a new job working at a Community Home, I found a gorgeous house close by where I became a lodger with a lovely young couple. Life was busy, hectic but fun! I had made some new friends, and we would take to going out into Ipswich on our days off, Clubbing, dancing, drinking, flirting, partying the night away till the early hours.

My days returning home were fewer, Cordelle and Violette had both met someone and had settled down, planning to live in America, so were quite busy preparing for this.

Mum and Dad seemed stuck in their dysfunctional world together, neither seeming happy but battling on nether the less. I knew they were not really getting on but even as an adult, you never think your mum and dad will split up. Well, they did!

I was at work and mum called my work phone. She sounded hysterical, crying her eyes out, begging for me to come home. She told me dad had taken a few bags of stuff and left her, telling her he had fallen in love with someone else. I promised I would head home as soon as I finished my shift. I called my sister, who said she would go and sit with her till I got there.

When I got there, mum was just sitting in dad's chair with a blanket round her sobbing and staring into space, repeating 'but I love him!'. I reassured her she will be ok, that we will help her through it. Ihelped her get into bed and I returned to the lounge, sitting in darkness, staring into nothingness, shocked, stunned by what happened, all quiet apart from hearing mum crying in the distance.

Dad later called me, saying how he cannot cope with mum's craziness anymore, that he had found someone who was amazing and beautiful and loved him for him. He refused to tell me where or who he was with, saying he was happy and not to worry.

Supporting mum with the break-up was difficult, she had sporadic outbursts of emotions, from uncontrollable grief, it felt like she was giving up, to huge outbursts of anger and rage.

One time, she asked I take her to see dad at his work, I tried to explain it was not a good idea, but she demanded I do so. When we got there, she told me to stay in the car, walking off into his office, to later return with dad at her heels, both shouting at each other, she turned round shouting right into his face, he swore at her;

she stopped for a moment then reached out her hand and slapped him in his face. For a split second; I froze as dad raised his hand and hit her in the face, shouting 'crazy bitch, go home,' looking at me and muttering 'take your fucking mother home!' walking off back into the office. I got mum into the car and drove her home. I called and informed my sister who went and supported dad as I supported mum.

Mum was devastated but it also seemed to be the last straw, for her to see and accept how the relationship was over.

After this, mum's anger drove her forward, she got all dad's belongings packed, demanding he collect them. It was like she had a splurge of energy from somewhere.

She started to mix more with people in the village, attending the local Women's Institute etc, had her hair cut into a pixie style, treated herself to a new wardrobe and really started to take more interest in her appearance. I returned to work with a little more hope that mum would be ok.

A few days of my return to work, I received a call from mum. She sounded so happy, excitable. Said dad had returned, had begged her back. I spoke to dad, who said he had made a big mistake and that he had come home. I was genuinely happy for them both, with slight trepidation and mistrust towards dad returning, concerned for mum more than anything.

I went to my family home that weekend, spending time with them, it all looked good, and they both seemed happier than I had seen them both in a long time. Mum seemed so contented, she was full of smiles, yet there was a nervous energy about her. I returned to Ipswich back to work, relieved I had been to see them both and praying they would continue to work out.

Things continued to tick along for a few more days, receiving bright and bubbly calls from mum, telling me all what they had been up to.

Then, the dreaded day came. I got a short, sharp text from dad, saying 'go be with your mum', no kiss, nothing. I called my mum, no answer, I managed to speak to my sister who said they had mum with her and how she was inconsolable. I went round there after my work shift. She was just sitting in an armchair, saying nothing, tears rolling down her cheeks. I sat beside her and wrapped my arms around her, holding onto her as she cried. She sobbed 'he doesn't love me; I may as well be dead!'

Apparently, dad had got up that morning, packed his things again, saying he does not and never has loved her and that he loves someone else, (one of his young secretaries) He had left before to be with her, but she had kicked him out after a row, which is when dad returned home wanting to try again. Well, this woman had changed her mind and wanted him back, had clicked her fingers and good old dad went running back.

I was devastated and so angry at him. We contacted mum's doctor, after an appointment with him, he prescribed mum strong anti-depressants and from what I can remember, sleeping tablets.

Mum stayed with my sister for a few days, whilst I continued to work. She then went back home; I visited her the next day. She hadn't even got dressed when I arrived, saying what is the point, and how she just kept repeating how she didn't want to be here anymore, crying uncontrollably. I tried to help as best I could, but it is so hard seeing your mother be broken so much she sees no hope. I didn't know what to say or do, felt so lost and hopeless.

I just showed her my love. Nan and

grandad arrived and took her to stay with them for a few days.

Despite all the love and support she was given, nothing seemed to work. The tablets seemed to numb her, the crying slowed down but instead, she took to just sitting in her chair staring into space. When nan and grandad brought her back home, I could see the concern in their eyes. Nan took me aside, saying she is still very low, doesn't want to talk about it etc. She asked if I could keep an eye on her. I could on my days off, but not when I am working. My sister was busy with two children and her husband, so we agreed we would all take it in turns to check in with her. I encouraged mum to go back to the doctors, but she refused, saying 'what's the point!''.

I returned to my home and went back to work. That night, I hardly slept, restless and worried for mum and what may happen to her, feeling desperate as

nothing I said or did seem to be helping.

The next day soon came. I was the nurse-in-charge that morning, it was a busy shift. My mobile rang as I was doing the drugs round, so I had to ignore it. The work's landline rang, another worker answered it, she held the handset, whispering over to me that my mum was on the phone and that I should speak to her. I quickly stopped what I was doing, locked the drugs cabinet and went to the phone. 'Oh, so now you CAN talk to your mother! About TIME! ' She shouted down the phone. I explained that I am the nurse-in-charge, that we are very busy today, hence why I hadn't answered my mobile. 'I am no good for anyone, just a nuisance!' sobbing uncontrollably. She then muttered amongst the sobbing, that she cannot cope anymore, that she is sorry she is no good for me and was only calling me to say goodbye. She then cut the phone; I could hear her crying hysterically

and loudly as she lowered the phone.

My heart was racing as I quickly called 999 to inform them, I believed my mum had taken an overdose. They wanted me to stay on the line till they got there but I had to complete the drugs round etc and try and get a replacement for me to I can head off to be with mum.

So, knowing the police and ambulance crew were going to turn up and break into my mum's/our family home at any moment, not sure if they will get there in time, I had to finish my shift as there was no cover available.

It was the longest day of my life. Every minute dragged, I felt sick inside, terrified I was going to lose my mum. I received a call from the ambulance saying that mum did not answer the door, that they had to force their way in, that she was unconscious but alive, she was now in the ambulance on the way to hospital.

I felt so guilty, felt I had let mum down, not being there for her as much as she needed, when things like this happens, you always question yourself and there is always the 'what ifs?'.

Mum eventually came round and was sectioned in hospital under The Mental Health Act, was in there for some weeks, not sure how long. I visited when I got time off work. It was awful seeing mum in that state, it was like she had given up, that without dad she was nothing, it made me so sad to see how her life had obviously revolved around him for so many years.

Throughout all of this, my dad carried on with his new life with his new lady. It was difficult and for the moment, I could not face seeing him.

When mum finally got discharged, she looked a bit better, she had lost weight, had her hair cut nice, even had some new clothes on. I could sadly, still see sadness in her eyes. She gave me a big hug, told me not to worry and went off to stay with nan and grandad.

Over the next few months, it was hard but mum slowly started to get better. She went to see a psychiatrist each month and started to go out more.

Mum started to be mum again, it was so amazing to see. She even came clubbing with my friends and myself, having a good time dancing the night away, staying at my then newly moved in flat. She became a regular visitor to the flat, which I loved so much! She got a beautiful kitten to keep her company, would bring her in her carry bag on the train to stay with us. So cute!

Thinking back to this time in my life, my we did have some fun! A couple of times she would join me when I took a disabled client, a lovely young lady out clubbing, they became good friends, and it was not long before Mum was always with us when we went anywhere.

One time, the three of us went to see The Chippendales, men dancing and stripping to undies on stage. At the end, they came off stage and all went to meet my client and mum, I never saw mum blush so much when they got her to pose in photos with them scantily clad besides her, their chests well oiled, she did not know where to put her face she said!

Mum really started to come out of herself, even said she was ready to think about dating! I helped her set up a profile on a dating site and it wasn't long until she got her first date. After several dodgy dates, mum met a lovely older man who she would later settle down with an marry.

Jake was a proud man, approx. 5ft 9, very thin, with grey wild hair, blue kind eyes and a lovely smile. He was a country man with a broad Norfolk accent. Dressed in greens and browns, with a tweed, peak cap. He smoked a pipe and I soon fell in love with this wonderful chatty man. He had served in the army and took pride in telling you all about what he used to do, had so so many stories to tell you, even if you were originally talking about something else, he always managed to get the conversation onto what we would call it 'during the war'! It was very endearing though.

After a few months of dating, they decided they would move in together, initially into Jakes' rented cottage. Once mum and dad's house were sold, mum and Jake used mum's divorce money to buy a beautiful town house in a small town. It was a lovely rickety old house, but with some work, they made it theirs. It became my second home.

Dad had also bought a house with his girlfriend, and all seemed good.

The divorce went through as well as it could do, with lots of gripes and mumblings from them both! That was soon put behind them and they all got on with their own lives.

After all the upheaval with my family going on, I had just done what I could to help my loved ones, be there for them but, in the process, I had forgotten about myself!!

4.

Ass A, The Heartbreaker

The Mind

Hidden in the deep grave of insanity
the pleasures that once came upon,
memories of love once asplendouring
happiness and joy now forgone

Shattered minds and broken hearts
whispers of incidences to blame,
showers of love and damages of lust
the remembrance, a memory of shame

The happiness that once spoke of life
the responsibility of actions a denial,
to think of one's love shown in such a way
to remember the love times so vial

The youthful times so fresh in my heart
to remember such actions deep in my soul,
a black cloud invading my once clear mind
shattered memories distinctly a whole

Darkness and clouds and black mists of pain
the moment of time such a gift of pure hell,
feeling such hatred and resentment for the one
that he is the reason my state of mind fell.

I was 22 years old, a qualified nurse, living in a beautiful studio apartment. It was filled with designer furniture, brightly coloured cushions and a massive piece of Kandinsky art asplendouring the chimney breast; I loved my little flat. I was doing well, qualified as a nurse, and getting pretty good money. Had a job I love, worked hard, and played hard.

On my days off, I went clubbing, dancing, and partying.

I met Ass A at a nightclub one night. He was with a friend of mine and we were introduced. He was tall, slightly chunky, afro hair cut short, wearing glasses that, to me, resembled milk bottles. He was dressed smart, with a sense of style. He smelled amazing and chewed gum, weird thing to remember! He held himself with an air of confidence, was well spoken and gave an impression of being a gentleman.

I was introduced to him, he nodded his head and then proceeded to observe me from afar as I danced and enjoyed the evening. I found him attractive, huge brown, smouldering eyes that looked right into me, like he had access to the depths of my soul. A slow song came on and he approached me, asking me to dance. As he was doing so and before I could answer, a girl came up to us, she grabbed one of his hands and dragged

him onto the dance floor. Then, I was forgotten as he grinded and moved with her along to the rhythm of the music. His hands were all over her.

I then spent the rest of the evening avoiding him, I could see he was a womaniser. My friend warned me off him, advising me to steer clear as she thought he was a heartbreaker. I agreed with the first impressions I had of him.

It was a few months later that I saw him again. I was out in the same club, with friends, feeling a little low as I was missing my partner.

Will was in the USAF and had been sent to work in Germany. I had found out today it was likely to be indefinitely, so I was unsure of our future.

As I was dancing, I spotted Ass A standing at the side of the dance floor, beer in his hand, watching me, staring at me.

I tried to ignore him, but everywhere I went, he seemed to be. He kept trying to catch my eye, but I avoided it.

He seemed attracted to my indifference, my lack of interest only seemed to spur him on and make him even more keen.

After a time, I decided there was no harm in talking to him. We spent a while talking, he was very charming, flattering and made me laugh. Once the conversation ceased, we went our separate ways. Towards the end of the evening, he returned and asked me to dance, and I agreed.

He took my hand and slowly led me to the dance floor. I tried to remain cool, but inside my heart was racing as I felt the warmth of his hand against mine. He took me into his arms, pulled me close to him and started to move to the music. I felt unsettled, a mixture of feelings, partly it felt nice, warm, and secure.

 However, also, despite my saying to myself 'no don't let him in, he will hurt you!', part of me felt excited feeling his body against mine, the smell of his musky aftershave, his whispering into my ear all heightening this feeling.

He behaved like a gentleman, was respectful and kind. He did all the right things, slowly my control slipped, and I started to like him. I think at the time, I thought maybe he could be just a good friend. We parted company after my giving him my phone number.

By the end of that week, he called me. He asked to meet up and we planned to go out for a drink. That night, when he came to pick me up, I sat inside my apartment, listening to him knocking on the door, then hearing his footsteps as he walked away. Something was stopping me, yet when he contacted me the next day, I felt bad and apologised, he surprised me with his patience,

I did this to him another two times, then I started to ignore his attempts to contact me. Eventually Ass A stopped the contact and I carried on with my life, but often thinking of him.

A few months later, I saw him in town. He waved at me, I smiled and waved back. The next day, he called me at work, we had a nice conversation and planned to meet. This time, I did open the door, something I later lived to regret.

We had a wonderful evening, a Thai meal. He behaved impeccably, was a gentleman, even wrapping his coat around me when we left the restaurant.

I subsequently ignored the 'womanising' warning signs I had seen at the start, enjoying his company and his flattery, agreeing to see him again when we parted ways, after he had reached forward and giving me a slow gentle kiss on my lips. I felt a rush of emotions and a spark igniting inside of me. It was after this

beautiful evening, that we started to see each other.

Not long after this, I received a call from Will; after many months of silence. He explained he had been working and had not had time to call (hard to believe) He expressed how much he loved me and subsequently proposed to me down the phone.

His plans were to return to America after he finished his time in the Air Force. I worked with a girl whose heart had been broken after marrying a USAF serviceman and was declined a Green Card to go to live in America, he was also refused to live here, they ended up divorcing. I thought of that and about how I would struggle leaving my family. I sadly declined his offer, hearing him cry broke my heart but I knew deep down, I was doing what was right for the both of us.

Six months later, Ass A and I were going strong. He was so calm and laid back, had a great sense of humour. He was not the most gorgeous man in the world, there was just something about him that mesmerized me, it was like I was under his spell.

It was not long after this, he suggested I move in with him. It just felt right to say yes. I moved into his home and for the next few months, despite the odd argument, everything seemed perfect. However, despite cleaning, decorating, and giving love to my new home, it just had a cold and disturbing aura about it. Something just didn't seem right. I never felt completely settled, bad auras and a dark presence envelope it.

Several months after moving in with him, I had just had a chest infection and had been on anti-biotics. Being new to starting the pill, I was not aware that the antibiotics would stop the pill from working. Not long after, I missed a period, took a test, and found out I was expecting. I call it a 'surprise', not a mistake. Despite our concerns regarding our financial circumstances, we were both happy with the news. However, I had to take some time out from him to think about my options. Our relationship had started to show signs of it not working; he was always out, could be short-tempered and had started to become controlling towards me. I stayed with my sister.

After a short time, we met and reached a decision to have our beautiful baby, I had nothing but excitement for the years ahead.

Although I was happy, I felt unnerved and unsettled. Something just didn't feel right in my head.

 Little did I know there was darkness behind his alluring smile. There were dark secrets inside of him, about his past, his family and other women. He would rarely discuss his childhood and only after me asking him about it, but I would just get a one sentences answer. I knew he had suffered a lot, we lived in his childhood family home that he bought off his father. Every bedroom had locks on, something I was curious as to why. He would make an excuse such as, 'just for privacy' but it somehow did not ring true. The longer I was with him, the more he talked. His dad got angry easily, Ass A often got the belt, also recalling a time he combed his afro hair with a fine-toothed comb, Ass A cried out as it hurt a lot, of which his father then beat him for being 'weak'.

His mum got killed in a car accident when he was younger, it seemed she was a loving soul, but he did not like to talk about her. His father remarried shortly after his wife's death and started a new family. From what I saw, he was very hard and sharp with Ass A, yet a loving and gentle man with his new young children. He had little time for his older son.

Ass A had siblings, all of them seeming to have issues in relationships, struggling to be able to give and receive love, Mark being the worst. He had a volatile relationship with his partner, was known to hit her, and 'keep her in line' as Ass A would say, apparently, she was just too 'mouthy'.

Ass A told me he had 2 children when he met me. 1 with different mothers, both of whom I spent a lot of time with. Beautiful little girls, who I soon grew to love. Happy memories of trips to London with the girls, going to Notting Hill Carnival and dancing the day away; so much fun and laughter as the girls tried to teach me to dance!

As I started to show signs of pregnancy, Ass A started to lose interest in me. It was like he loved me but just could not handle the commitment.

He started staying out till late at night, most nights and being snappy if I tried to talk to him about it.

Sexually, though, he could not get enough. Despite my pregnancy, he craved me, wanted me, desired me. He seemed to enjoy how my breasts were growing and got off touching them. It became like an obsession.

He would appear loving and tender, he had a way of making me feel beautiful, special, and sexy. After, he would want to completely wrap himself around me, holding me until he fell asleep. Special moments that would mislead me into thinking things could only get better from now onwards, but this was short-lived. As soon as he awoke each day, the coldness returned, and my heart would sink.

The late nights continued. I became increasingly concerned that maybe he just was not happy being with me. When questioned, he would be dismissive.

The longer this occurred, the more upset I was getting and that was when the aggression started. It started with the verbal aggression, shouting, name calling. Then came pushing me around, laughing as I cried, calling me 'psycho, just like your mum!'

The longer we were together, the worse he became. Nothing I did was good enough, I was 'useless' and 'no good'. He would often compare me to other women, hinting maybe he should go elsewhere as I obviously was not happy.

I was working as a nurse, it was quite a walk to get there, as I was getting more and more pregnant, I would struggle the journey. On a good day, I would be allowed the car, or he would give me a lift, but on a bad day, he would just laugh and tell me I deserve nothing, that I must walk 'you bitch.'

The aggression increased. Most nights, he would drink cans and cans of Tenants

Extra, the more he had, the nastier he seemed to be. The pushing became harder, he enjoyed hearing me cry out, would smile, and laugh.

One time, he pushed me when I was at the top of the stairs, I fell back and managed to turn around, so I fell forwards, still landing a few steps down onto my belly. I laid on the floor, feeling like the wind had been blown out of me. Ass A just laughed, stepped over me saying 'yeh lay there bitch, where you deserve!!' and went out on his nightly jaunt.

Several occasions, he would push me against the corner of a table, the edge hitting me in my tummy.

Grabbing me, pushing me against the wall, screaming into my face. Silly things angered him.

I was getting tired easily with work and being pregnant. Sometimes, I felt so fatigued, I would lie down and fall asleep, not able to cook dinner or clean the house. He expected food ready as soon as he arrived from work. Any discrepancies or times I was too tired, I would be punished, mood depending upon what my punishment was.

I developed a way of coping to keep me and our unborn baby safe and to prevent any drama; by not reacting to him when he was in one of his moods, not challenging him when I was upset or angry at him.

Developing this way of being felt to me a weakness and it only made me feel more weak and unworthy as a person and as a woman.

I became like a robot, being controlled and manipulated by him, deep down I was broken and scared; craving his love but also wanting to leave and be free at the same time.

I did not have the capability or strength to leave him at this point, leaving an abusive relationship is not as simple or easy as one may think.

I bled a lot though out my pregnancy, not helped by the bruising he caused to my belly and the number of times I would fall onto my tummy after he pushed me. I was constantly on edge, anxious, scared I may lose our baby I had grown to love and long to be born. I guess because of this fear, I tolerated what was happening, I knew my baby and I would be safer that way.

I did try and leave three times during my pregnancy. Only to be lured back home to him, after he made false promises and claimed undying love.

I had no money saved, was helping him pay his mortgage arrears off as he promised once I did that, he could add me to the deeds and mortgage. I felt helpless and that I had nowhere to go.

By this point, he had beaten me down not just physically, but emotionally. I had no self-worth or confidence; I did not think I would be able to cope alone.

Ass A had issues re possessiveness and jealousy. He did not tolerate me having male friends.

One friend I had, he threatened him when he had some flower delivered for me when I was really struggling with morning sickness. He called me later the same day to check how I was feeling, Ass A answered the phone, he was very rude, saying how dare he send his partner flowers, that if he continued, he would go over to his and beat his ass.

Although he had suffered racism in the past, including recently at work, he did not like black African men, said they 'smelt'. He was disgusted that I had two black African friends and used his aggression to scare me and stop me seeing them, warning me if I continued to see him, there would be trouble, that I would be to blame for what he did.

If I went to see friends, he would demand to know who I was meeting, where and times. I would be on edge whilst out, checking the time so I was sure to be back home on time, to prevent him kicking off.

You may wonder why I put up with all this? Love? He controlled me? Domestic Violence? Fear? So many things, but I think the emotional abuse had really started to knock me, affect me, to the point he had power and control over me.

Although he did not like me having male friends, it appeared he had a different rule for himself! Ass A continued to go out at night till all hours, returning the next morning. I also received numerous phone calls from different women, most claiming to be seeing him, some evening claiming to be the mother of a child I did not know about. When I told him, he would laugh, turning it all around on me, accusing me of lying, calling me 'Psycho' and 'possessive'. That I would lose him if I continued in this way.

The nine months of carrying our baby were lonely and traumatic, I attended all the health appointments alone as he was 'too busy'. He showed little interest in our unborn child or me.

When I went into labour, my mum and stepdad came to hospital with me, and Ass A met us there. He sat reading the New Testament and did not speak, no reassurance or love shown to me. It felt like he was there because he had to be, not that he wanted to be. Labour was difficult, with complications meaning the Font Ouse method being used to deliver him.

My beautiful son was born, I was overjoyed. (Note I say 'my son'. Throughout Jerrys' life, Ass A has not really bothered much, mostly let him down.

He has not played the part of a father, I brought Jerry up as a single-parent, despite my efforts for his dad to play a part in his life, so hence the saying 'my son'.)

He was 7lb 7ozs, all legs, dark blue eyes like sapphires and black silky hair with curly locks covering his forehead.

Beautiful tanned complexion, he looked perfect, like a porcelain doll.

Ass A appeared happy, held him, and posed for photos. As soon as that was done, he could not get out quick enough. Apparently, he was going out to 'wet the baby's head'. (I later found out he wet his head and met an ex and slept with her, the night Jerry was born.)

I was so happy about my son being born, yet this was overshadowed with my doubts and fears over Ass A's stability and loyalties.

When I was discharged from hospital, I was advised to rest as I had stitches.

Ass A promised he would look after me and Jerry but this, sadly lasted but a day.

I was soon expected to fulfill my 'duties' in the home, as a mother, housekeeper, cook and partner, as well as heal. If I did not meet his expectations, he would compare me to other women, call me a 'useless, no-good mother', that maybe he should 'replace' me and laugh.

He loved nothing more to say all this and ridicule me when we had visitors, he was never brave enough though to say it in front of my family.

All the emotional abuse I was receiving really took its toll on me. I became very nervous and paranoid. I was also exhausted as Jerry was not a good sleeper.

I felt useless as a mother, starting to believe the things he had said to me. I started to show signs of depression, resorting to withdrawing into myself and being tearful, a lot.

Ass A had no patience and just dismissed me as being 'Psycho', 'useless', 'no good', 'weak', 'bad mother' etc which only made me feel worse. His late-night outings continued, and he started to not come home at all at night.

Ass A belonged to the Territorial Army and two weeks after Jerry was born, he went away with them, working.

During that time, Jerry fell out of his sling (the sling arm broke), whilst I was trying to stop him falling headfirst onto concrete, I grabbed hold of his arm, subsequently causing him to have a greenstick fracture. I called his dad, he refused to come home, just shouting down the phone, calling me the usual names and how ashamed he was of me doing such a terrible thing, abusing our son.

When he finally returned home, things only seemed to get worse. If I behaved, did everything he wanted, everything was good, he was attentive and loving.

He was very demanding sex wise; I was breastfeeding, and he seemed to get turned on watching me feed our son. Waiting till Jerry finished feeding, telling me to put him into the cot, I would try and explain he shouldn't be laid down on a full tummy, Ass A would shout 'do it womaaaan, stop fussing!'.

He would then take me into our bedroom and relieve himself in the way he wanted, whether I wanted it or not was out of the question. If I did not give him what he wanted or behaved as a 'no good womaaan!', I would get punished, usually verbally and emotionally, I was scared to stand up for myself, so would submit, more for my son's sake than my own safety.

He continued his nights out, often saying he is working late. Sometimes I would try and call him at work to see what take away he needed; his work mates would tell me he left hours ago. I knew that something just was not right.

One evening, I asked my friend to call his work and see if he was still working, I was too upset that night to do it myself. His work mate who answered, guessed it was not by me as knew me, he asked who she was, when she explained why she was calling, he opened up to her.

He said how awful he thought it all was, that we had a beautiful baby boy together and there he is playing around. That he knows what he is doing, that he leaves at 8pm, often goes out dressed up, and will joke to people that he is on a promise. That they all knew what he was up to.

When Ass A finally returned home that night, I could tell he had been drinking, he was staggering and fell into his armchair in the lounge, with a beer in his hand. I told him what had happened.

Again, he became angry, shouting, saying someone at work obviously had it in for him. That it is all rubbish and how

I do not trust him because I was an 'insecure Psycho bitch!'. He got himself a beer, took a big swig, then started to pace the corridor as he was yelling at me. I started to cry and I recall him laughing at me, saying 'look at the state of you, pathetic!'. He again proceeded to swig his beer.

He then said 'no wonder people cheat when they have a no good womaaan and mother like you! Ha ha ha !'. I started crying more, I leant towards him, taking his beer saying I just wanted him to talk to me so we can sort it out. Please stop drinking! We cannot go on like this!' He jumped up, lunged at me, trying to hit me, grabbed at the beer in my hand, swearing and hurling more and more insults.

My heart was racing, sweat dripping off my forehead. He then said 'Well you can fucking leave if you don't like it. But you know if you leave me, the boy stays here. Because you are psycho, you will get restricted access! Cos you are mentally ill bitch.' I screamed loudly and in what I think was frustration, I hit at the wall, forgetting the bottle was still in my hand. Blood started to spurt from my hand, and I fell to the floor crying my eyes out. He just laughed, then called for an ambulance.

I remember the rubbish that came out of his mouth as he spoke on the phone. How I am very unwell, unstable, and unsafe being in the community. That I had just gone to attack him and then self-injured my hand with a bottle.

I was taken to a and e. After having my wound dressed, an official looking man came to talk to me. So many questions, that my head got in a muddle, so I just cried. He advised me I have Post-Natal Depression, prescribed me some tablets, and sent me home with a psychiatrist appointment.

When I arrived back home, Ass A looked so disappointed saying I had fooled their head. I went to bed, crying myself to sleep, feeling trapped, not wanting to be there, knowing things were bad but too scared to leave. Scared I may lose my son.

Having depression and being brainwashed by him, I had no confidence or self-belief. I even started to believe that everything happening was all my fault like he said. I hated myself physically and mentally. He had full control, if I went out, I would have to be back for a set time to prepare tea, he expected things at a certain time. Friends started to notice by my anxiety re time, but I was too scared to confide in them.

I was literally just existing for my son. Behaving like a zombie, it was the only way to cope, not feel, not think.

Life ticked on by, my head in a turmoil, wanting to flee but too scared to, so instead, I tried to make my baby's first

year of life a treasured and happy one.

On my days free, I would take Jerry out, sometimes with friends or family, sometimes alone. I have so many beautiful memories of sitting on the beach, going to zoos, swimming, walking in the countryside. They were wonderful times, but times Jerry and I spent together, without his dad joining in; he showed little interest in either Jerry or myself. I became compliant, more like a robot, my mind controlled by him.

He seemed content with this. We spent some weekends going out, spending time together, often with his beautiful two daughters, Kerry and Catherine. I started to become happier during these times,

Ass A put on a good show for his girls, not wanting them to see the 'real' him. It was like Jerry and myself were show pieces, to make him look good. He would only show interest in us if the girls were round, if there were visitors or we

bumped into someone he knew when we were out.

Jerry was known as 'the boy' by him. He showed little interest. I started to savor the good times, battling on and playing the dutiful girlfriend, trying hard to make him happy. To prevent anymore arguments and confrontations.

He seemed happier but would still go out some nights till early hours. Sometimes, when he came home, he would want me, if I was awake, I would let him, by this point, I had a low self-image, he made me think that, so it was difficult wanting him to touch me, why would he want to when I was so ugly. The worst would be if I was asleep. He would not wake me, choosing instead to just help himself.

I would awaken to pain inside me, he had entered me, pushed his member into me, whilst I was dry, he went on and on, ignoring my cries to stop, it felt so uncomfortable, but it seemed the more I

protested, the more he got turned on and the harder he pumped.

One night, when I could take no more, things came to a head. It had got to the point, at night if he did not come home after work, or on a weekend, I would nervously lie in bed waiting.

That night, I could not sleep, my head was whirling, I did still love him, why was I not enough for him when all I did was try and please him? I sat at the bottom of the stairs crying, sobbing helplessly.

When he arrived, I asked him where he had been, he muttered 'out' and 'none of your business bitch!'. He pushed me out of the way and went upstairs. As he walked past me, I saw a red mark on the collar of his white shirt, what looked like lipstick. It had gotten to the point that I knew he was seeing someone.

I had started to receive calls to the house, different girls would ring, asking

for him, demanding to know who I am, then cutting the phone after I explained.

I knew he was lying to me. I followed him into our bedroom, all I wanted to do was talk with him calmly, for him to own up, so I could see I wasn't going mad after all.

He refused to talk to me, 'I have come home, you should think yourself lucky! What more do you want?!'. I became angry, all the times of being treated like this had built up, I exploded. I started to shout 'why, why? You have a beautiful family, why do this? I try so hard; I love you and you treat me like a piece of shit!'.

He just laughed. He called me psycho, possessive, clingy, too much, enough for any man to refuse to stay, to find someone else the way I was.

I started to cry, sobbing, 'Look at you! You are pathetic, weak, you are a no good woman! No good mum, you are useless!

Psycho bitch. I have had it up to here with you and your psycho ways! That is it! Maybe I should go and do what you keep accusing me of?' he got up from the bed and tried to leave the room. I was standing in the doorway crying, he grabbed me and pushed me onto the bed, kissing me, groping me roughly saying he will make it up to me. I tried to get him off, had to be forceful pushing him back off me. He shouted 'Right, I am going to put a stop to all this. Then you will leave me alone!'

He left the room, I could hear him pulling the loft ladder down, all I could think was he was getting a suitcase, that he was going to leave us. I lay there sobbing, feeling like I had lost part of myself, not being able to cope with the despair and heartache I was feeling.

He soon returned. He stood leaning against the door frame, smiling proudly. He lifted his arm and I saw he was holding one of his guns in his hand. He loaded it quietly in front of me, all the time staring at me, smiling.

He then proceeded to spend I think two hours walking round the house with it, waving it around laughing, pointing it at me, at one point holding it to his head saying would I like that? I sat up, tried to get the gun off him, saying 'please stop!'. He pushed me back, hitting me repeatedly on my body with the loaded gun, he then lifted it and pointed it at my forehead. I froze, laid on the bed, motionless, terrified.

Ass A appeared to be highly excited, but seemed disappointed as I was not reacting how he wanted.

He left the room, saying 'this will do it! Bitch'. He lent down, picked up the landline phone, trying to yank the lead out of the wall, throwing the phone onto the floor. He walked off laughing.

I heard him open Jerry's bedroom, panic rose inside of me. I jumped up, runninginto the hallway. He was standing over his cot, with his gun in his hand, smiling.

I begged him to leave his room and come and speak to me. He slowly lifted his arm and lowering the gun, so it was aimed at our beautiful baby's head. I froze, all I could hear was my heart racing. Ass A said quietly, he can do what he wants, he is in charge. That Jerry is his son, and he decides what he will do. I was terrified he was going to shoot him. I felt all the blood drain from my head, I felt giddy but remained standing, calmly and quietly saying

'Yes you are his daddy, and he loves you. Hurt me but not our beautiful boy, your boy.' I said no more and waited for him to respond. He spent a few moments looking at Jerry, watching him sleep, then proceeded to lift his arm out of the cot andwalked out of his room. He stared at me coldly as he walked past, with such hatred in his eyes, and slowly walked downstairs. I closed Jerry's bedroom door quietly and sat down in the hallway.

It was then it hit me, how in danger we were, what could happen, how Ass A was prepared to shoot me, kill me. I felt relief and thanked God that Jerry slept through it all, even when his dad held the gun at his head, his own daddy doing such an evil thing, to him, an innocent little baby.

As I sat there on the landing at the top of the stairs, I looked and saw the landline upstairs phone was on the floor besides me, still where it had landed when Ass A had thrown it. The phone cable was hanging from the plug socket, most of the wire was broken, but my heart started to race as I noticed there was a piece of wire still connected in the plug and into the socket.

I quietly picked up the phone, holding the handset to my ear. I could hear a dialling tone. I dialled my friend's number and quietly told her I must be quick, begging her to come urgently and wait in the car for me. She started to ask why, what had Ass A done, why was I whispering etc. By this time, he had heard me and had started to come up the stairs. As he reached the top, I spoke loudly 'Please come get us! Hurry, park down to road, we will come to you. Do NOT come into the house, please hurry, I beg you!' She replied she will call the police, that something is not right. Ass A yelled loudly, screaming 'You bitch, what have you done?!' he pulled the phone from my grasp and throwing it aside. He pushed me towards the stairs, yelling 'Move!' I sat down, begged him to put the gun down of which he said he would when he feels safe, and I have calmed down.

He returned downstairs. I again tried the phone and called my friend back; she said the police are on their way.

I sobbed, whispering 'he has a gun!' She replied she will call the police back and tell them. He again heard me, shouted 'bitch' and ran up the stairs, pointing the gun at me, I screamed and threw the phone down, shouting 'I am sorry I am sorry'.

He grabbed me by my arm and took me downstairs. He went into the lounge sitting in his armchair. I sat at the bottom of the stairs.

There was silence for what seemed like forever. After what seemed a long time, I told him quietly and calmly that my friend had called the police. That they were coming and would likely arrest him. It would be better for him if he just gave himself up rather than fight it. He took in a deep breath, sighed loudly, and told me to call them, it was then he finally put the gun down.

I called the police, whilst sitting on the stairs and Ass A was still in his armchair.

They asked me questions and gave me guidance on what to do next. That I must go and get Jerry, wrap him in a blanket and then come out of the back door. I was told to bring nothing but Jerry and no coat. They told me to walk out quietly and slowly.

As I opened the back door, it was still dark, but lights were coming from past the gate. As I walked down the garden path, I saw red dot lights on my body, as I looked for the source, I could see shadows of people crouched down. (I later found out it was soldiers with guns.)

I was told to walk out into the car park. I could see numerous police vehicles and a few black vans; it was all so scary and overwhelming.

I also saw my neighbor returning home but not allowed past the cordon they had put up. He looked at me with pity in his eyes, I put my head down, wishing I could hide myself with shame.

There were police waiting for me who helped me into their police car and took me and Jerry to the local police station.

The police took I believe approximately three hours talking to Ass A on the phone. I think they were doing it till he came down off the adrenaline and testosterone rush he had been on and to wait for him to tire.

He was then asked to go out the back door with his hands up. He recalled later, how, when he did so, he could also see red dots on his body, he was then grabbed, put in handcuffs, and taken to a police car. He saw many people dressed in black holding guns, aimed at him. When he was arrested, he suffered much humiliation (so he said later). They searched him and were quite rough, they shouted questions rapidly demanded immediate answers from him.

He was then taken to the police station, then strip and internally searched and put into a cell till the morning when he was then questioned. They searched our house for guns and bullets, soon finding it all in the loft.

They found the gun and the bullets in the lounge besides his armchair on the floor. The saddest thing of all was, later the police told me the bullets in the gun were blanks, that if he had held it close to me and shot, it could still have injured me, but obviously not as seriously as real bullets. I felt sick inside, all what he did that night was to wind me up, it was sick!!

Jerry and I were at the station all night. Poor Jerry was amazing, we laid a coat on the table, laying him on it with his shawl on top of him. He slept most of the night, to my relief. I remember one of the police went to the hospital and got me some nappies, they were excellent really and so good with me.

They had to ask me to remove my clothes to check for any injuries, especially from when he had beaten me with the gun for bruising where he had beaten me with the gun. I had bruises down my leg and chest and arms.

They asked me to stand in this room whilst they took photos. They questioned me and did my statement with me.

When it was over, they asked if I wanted to press charges. Knowing what Ass A was like, I just couldn't do it, I was terrified what he would do next.

He had threatened to take our son away from me and I just could not risk losing my baby. So, I had to say no.

They took us home, advising us to leave Ass A as what he did was unacceptable, they told me about Women's Refuges, but I was in so much shock, I could not retain anything they said.

When we got back, I thanked them for all their help and headed to the house.

I visited my GP, telling him what happened. He gave me sedatives, I went home, put Jerry to bed, took my tablets and fell asleep. Later I awoke to Jerrys' crying, I changed his nappy and got back into bed, laying there, fully clothed, just staring into the darkness, nothingness. That was how I stayed throughout the morning until I finally fell asleep again.

I awoke to the door going, it was his father. I let him in, he made me a coffee and sat with me whilst I got Jerry up and got him fed and ready for the rest of the day. His dad was supportive to me but also quite dismissive with what had happened, trying to brush it aside, life goes on kind of thing. Saying how we need to talk, not fight, how was what happened to me fighting?

I was too ashamed to tell mum and dad. Even when it went on the news on tv and mum rang asking if it was me, I said no. I did not want her to worry.

When Ass A was released and he came home, his dad took him down the pub. Not one of them asked how I was, it was like he got the support, that I was the one in the wrong.

They later came back; I got a half-hearted apology. It was like he had been told to do it. Later he did become emotional, saying how he would lose his gun license and likely be kicked out of the TA, but it was more he was sorry for himself. I explained how I cannot go on like this, it all must stop, the late nights out, his temper etc. If he wanted me and Jerry in his life, he needed to start making an effort. He agreed he would. Thinking on it now, he did not really show any remorse for what happened, and the sorry was later found to be unmeant.

I finally told mum and dad, I lied to make it look better, that ASS A had been very low, was now under the doctor and going to help, but it was all rubbish.

I just felt so weak and desperate, I did not want them to be disappointed in me. Mum was amazing and her new husband, they were very supportive, coming to see me and Jerry regularly, checking I was Ok.

Things got better, he started to try, spending more time with us, it was like we were a proper family. We went on holiday, went out on day trips and generally built up some beautiful memories of our family.

I started to relax and feel happy again. Jerry prospered in the secure setting he was now growing up in, growing well, reaching all his milestones for his age. I felt so proud and happy. But sadly, it did not last very long.

Even when it was ok, I would sometimes catch him looking at me, with such hatred, then he would smile at me. It was like the quiet before the storm. I felt so trapped and started to wonder if it

was worth it.

One weekend, Ass A said he was going to take in his brother's dog, Shadow, as he did not want him anymore. He did not check if I was ok with it, drove to London and picked it up. Sad thing is I don't know why he got him, because he shut him in the downstairs toilet and hardly bothered with him. I felt so sorry for the poor dog.

Not long after, my sister's cat had kittens and she gave one to Jerry. We named him Tigger and little Jerry loved him. It was so sweet seeing them together; Tigger would cuddle up with Jerry and fall asleep together.

Ass A introduced Tigger to Shadow and I knew straight away Shadow did not like him. He was on his lead but licked his lips, scratching and pulling to get to the poor kitten.

I was also concerned how Shadow was with Jerry, he seemed unsure of him, he was quite a nervy dog. Shadow bonded with Ass A, but not with me. I tried to take him for walks with Jerry in his pram, but he just pulled, completely ignoring me growling and snarling at people we walked past. I knew if he got off his leash, he would likely turn on someone. I couldn't blame the poor dog, his early years had been full of abuse and beatings, he did not know how to behave and probably didn't like humans very much.

Poor Shadow continued to be kept in the toilet but let out to run out the front each day, Ass A ignoring my concerns over his aggression. And laughing when he would chase our older cat, Jake.

One day, I came home from shopping, Ass A had stayed at home with Jerry. I entered the house and could hear growling in the next room. I went into the lounge, Jerry was in his bouncer chair with Tigger laying on him, Ass A in his armchair, watching Shadow who was sitting next to him snarling at Tigger. I quickly said, 'please put him away, he will go for him.' He replied 'sshh womaaaan they need to work out who is boss!'. But Tigger was only a kitten and Shadow was a muscley and stocky Staff! Next thing Shadow ran to where Jerry was, picking Tigger up in his teeth taking him into his mouth. Jerry started crying and screaming, holding his hands out, sobbing. Shadow snarled at him, and all Ass A could do was laugh. All you could see was poor Tigger's back legs hanging out of Shadow's mouth Shadow snarling and dribbling. I shouted at Shadow, 'stop!' He ignored me till eventually Ass A punched him in his jaw and he released the poor kitten. Tigger survived but was never the same again, nervy and terrified of dogs.

Despite the attack, Ass A refused to get rid of Shadow. Even after he started to snap at me when I tried to feed him.

I was by this time, terrified for my baby but knew I couldn't say anymore as I would likely get hit.

Ass A returned to the way he was before, but worse. He continued pushing me about if I did not behave as he wanted. When he got angry, he would remind me how he forgave me for putting him in a police cell for 24 hours and how lucky I was.

I had returned to work, and my manager was aware of my situation at home. She was very supportive, started mentoring me, helping to raise my confidence and self-esteem.

Just before Christmas, one afternoon, the back door went. When I opened the door, an official looking man stood there. It was a Social Worker who had come to see how Jerry was, after what had happened. Ass A was not there, so I had the chance to talk to him and offload.

He warned me if the violence continued and any further police involvement, I could be at risk of losing Jerry. I told him I was not happy and was considering leaving him. The Social Worker left happy with how Jerry was developing and that he felt I was keeping him safe. That visit shook me, terrified me. I started thinking about my options and talked it through with my manager.

The icing on the cake came when we went on a family holiday to Greece. Ass A flirted with other women the whole week, spent all our holiday money on himself, so I had to ask a couple I made friends with lend me some so I could buy us food it was so embarrassing! Ass A had no shame, he didn't care how he looked.

On return home, mum and my stepdad came over to see us. He was at work. Mum asked to see photos, I decided to get the video camera as he had recorded a lot on holiday.

I set it up and we started watching it just as he returned from work. He protested saying he had not edited it yet. But it was too late. Soon, we all realised why he was panicking; the video was full of topless women with Ass A flirting with them. I had had enough by now.

Not long after this, I went to work, spoke to my boss, Maggie, who advised Jerry and myself would be best going into a refuge. I agreed, so she got on the phone and sorted it for me. The next day, when Ass A was at work, I got my stuff, packed what I needed for Jerry, and we left him. We moved into a local refuge.

Refuge life was hard, it was meant to be a safe haven and to a point, it was. However, I was the only woman that worked so was out a lot, Jerry at the child carers. So, I didn't get much time to bond with the others. I shared a small room with two other families, Jerry had a travel cot besides my bed.

The other mums smoked weed, even in the bedroom whilst Jerry was sleeping. When I tried to say something, I just got laughed at with comments like I think I am special because I work. Although I worked, I had little money as one thing I did not tell you was that he also financially abused me, saying he was struggling, had to pay for his two children and had mortgage arrears, so I had been paying for everything, getting myself into debt because of it.

Two nights after I moved into the refuge, Ass A called me, crying, saying he missed us and loved us both. He asked if he could see Jerry which I agreed. He picked him up and I was to get him from the house, but I said I would park in the car park. He came out to the car without Jerry, saying he is sleeping, begging me to come into the house to talk. He looked calm and as Jerry was sleeping, I agreed.

As soon as I walked through the back door, he grabbed me, trying to kiss me roughly. I could hear Jerry crying. I pushed Ass A away and ran upstairs to get him. As I was standing in the nursery picking him up, Ass A came in, shouting how dare I push him away. I put Jerry back down and calmly asked Ass A to let you get Jerry ready so we can leave. He pushed me against the wall, bashing my head repeatedly on it. He stared at me, saying 'you deserve everything you get!' and went downstairs. I got Jerry ready and left the house.

That was the last time I saw Ass A in our house, knowing it was just too dangerous and not fair on Jerry seeing all the abuse I was suffering. What will that teach a young child?

I allowed Ass A to continue seeing Jerry, but sadly this didn't last long as he proceeded to use seeing Jerry as an excuse to seeing me and abusing me further.

He would pick up and drop off Jerry two roads away from the refuge I was staying in; this was due to that no-one must know where the refuges are especially perpetrators. Funny though, he knew where we were staying as told me the second day I was there, at the time I was baffled how he knew.

Whilst I was in the refuge, I still worked and had started at university, evening classes, doing my conversion from Enmh to Rnmh nursing. Ass A would text and call my mobile a lot. I would ignore him, but if he did that, he would resort to calling me at work.

One day, when he called, he begged me back, when I said no, he then threatened to go to the Child Carers and steal Jerry. Another time, he threatened to kill us both. I was too scared to call the police, so carried on with my life, but explaining to the child carer they must not allow him to collect Jerry, of which they agreed.

The last time I allowed access, he was due to return him, and I was waiting in the usual drop off point. He pulled up, getting out of the car. He came up to me, said how this cannot go on, I need to admit how wrong I am, that my psycho ways caused all this. That if I apologised, he would take me back. I refused to, asking if he can unlock the car so I could get Jerry. He said, 'no you listen bitch!' He then started to punch me repeatedly in the chest, calling me bitch as he did so. I could see Jerry screaming and holding his arms up to me in the car. I begged Ass A to stop and to let me get our son as he is crying. He laughed, saying 'well I don't think you deserve him; you are a no good mum. You are not safe to have a child! Say bye bye to him!' he got into the car and sped off down the road, laughing.

That moment, I felt all the blood drain from my body, I fell onto my knees and screamed. People came running to me, asking me what's wrong, I couldn't speak, my mouth had gone dry, I managed to blurt out 'my son!'. I sobbed and sobbed feeling like my whole world had ended. I tried to call Ass A and sent messages begging him to return Jerry, I was so desperate I apologised for anything I had done to upset him.

For what seemed like forever, Ass A's car came hurtling down the road, he opened the door shouting 'take him, but I am warning you, next time you start, I will not come back!' I got Jerry and as soon as I shut the car door, Ass A sped off down the road.

After that, I spoke to my Refuge Worker and I decided Ass A was not safe to see our son, I sent him a message explaining that, saying if he wanted access, it would need to be through a children's centre. He did not respond, and all went quiet for a month or so.

The refuge supported me to apply for

social housing, due to being made homeless after suffering Domestic Violence.

It took a few months but then got an offer for a little council house. We had a look round, it looked like a nice area but needed painting, plus I had no furniture.

My friend Martin offered to contact Ass A and arranged for him and myself to go to the house and collect Jerry and my belongings, whilst Ass A was at work. I will never forget the day we moved out, Martin sitting on the edge of the loft, legs dangling down. Whilst clearing it, he found a lit area at the back. After looking closer, he found lots of cannabis plants, obviously another source of Ass A's income for his luxurious life style.

Even after doing this, I was left with Jerry's furniture for his nursery, a duvet for myself and bedding. The council gave me a voucher for paint but nothing else. It was assumed as I worked part-time,

I had money, but those on benefits got money to furnish their homes. I was still struggling and had hardly any money after paying my debts I had accrued.

I resorted to charity shops and a fantastic agency called The Furniture Project. I told them my circumstances and they helped me so much, reducing prices etc, even giving me some items for free.

On the day we moved, my mum and stepdad helped. I was so excited to start a new life, me and Jerry. I felt safe, knowing Ass A did not know where I was moving to. Sadly, that night, as I put Jerry to bed, I saw a light in the back garden, I looked out of the window and there he was sitting there on a bench, smoking a cigarette, waving up at me. He then stood up, walked round the front to the car and drove off. I called the police who said they would go and speak with him. There were no more late-night visits to my garden after that.

He had other ways to hurt and punish me for leaving him though. Such as stopping maintenance payments when I had stopped the child access, using Jerry to get to me. Trying to make me feel guilty for denying our son his father.

Also, I had two catalogues whilst I lived with him. He rang up huge debts with both, buying things for himself and some women's clothes. I was in so much debt, I often could not afford to eat.

It got to a point, that I could not even afford to buy food for Jerry so had to resort to asking Ass A for help. This was yet another way for him to regain control.

The only way he would help would be if I allowed him to come over, to see his son he would say. After approximately thirty minutes playing with him, he would then turn his attention to me. He felt I should earn his support, and I was so desperate, I allowed him to kiss and grope me, all so I could feed my son. I felt violated, a a sick feeling inside me. Ashamed, so so ashamed but it was the only source of help I could get.

He would demand to have Jerry overnight, I allowed it one time, only for poor Jerry to be dropped off in a filthy nappy and so thirsty. The other times he planned to have him, I would pack Jerry a bag and he would sit at the bottom of the stairs, excitedly waiting for his dad. But Ass A did not bother to turn up. Then I would have to explain to Jerry this, he would often cry, I would wipe his tears off his cheeks, kiss him and tell him how sorry I was, that daddy was just busy.

At night, Jerry would sit on his knees and ask me to help him pray. He would ask 'for daddy to come soon' and also pray for everyone in the world to be happy. He had such a kind, pure heart.

My heart ached seeing him hurt. It got to a point Ass A let him down more than he saw him; I could not bear seeing poor

Jerry get hurt, so I had to put a stop to it all.

The violation and inappropriate behaviour continued until I could not go any longer, as well as the terrible way he was treating our son, hurting him so much. I spoke to my manager, who again supported me, advising I have a benefits review. Thank goodness I did as I got granted a small amount of housing benefit plus child and working tax credit.

I contacted Ass A, this time taking control and prepared to deal with the back lash, calling the police if I needed to. I had had enough of being a doormat! I told him I was not prepared to be an emotional or physical punch bag for him or have to sell myself so he will support our son. That any further contact will only be able to occur at a Child Contact Centre, that I am not prepared to put our son in the middle of his abusive ways anymore.

This time I stuck to what I said, but

but Ass A said he would never see his child in such a place, that he would fight me in court. I waited for the day, but it never came!

Sadly, Jerry became affected by his father's behaviour. He started to have tantrums, had difficulty sleeping and was very clingy with me. The less he saw of his father, the more stable he seemed to become, even though it saddened me that his dad was not really bothered about our beautiful son.

I concentrated on my son, on my work and having a good life, consistent routine for poor Jerry. He soon started to thrive; life became good again!

5.

The Destroyer
The Touch

To feel this dreadful thing
to know that certain moment,
the evil inside of him
a wondrous thought of torment

To know the time has come
his possessed touch around me,
to pray for blessing of one
self-pity and disgust surround me

To forget who one is
thus being with no soul,
the matter occurring to me
not seeing as a whole

To feel the haunt of his desire
this filling me with shame,
one knowing his pleasures are afire
to feel oneself to blame

To know one's hatred still goes on
the years are passing by,
to feel the memories, the time upon
to wish it was a lie

To hate oneself for all the past
to feel oneself to blame,
to hope that this will never last
that gives me so much pain.

Life had become good, Jerry was growing into a funny, mischievous, wacky little lad. Curious and inquisitive with life. A big zest for life and wackily cute like his mum.

I continued my work as a Nurse. Long hours working so I could afford to pay all the bills and give Jerry a good life. Whilst I worked, Jerry would go to a child minder, then Pre-School.

He was such a chatty little thing, happy and spritely. He would spend some holidays with his nan and grandpa; they spoilt him rotten. Taking him camping, trips out, dinosaur land, seaside, zoos etc. He always really looked forward to going on adventures with them, his little bags packed, waiting patiently for them to arrive, squealing with delight when he saw their car pull up. They were amazing grandparents and loved Jerry deeply.

I made the most of my days off with Jerry. I did not have much money, but always

found something to do; walks, bike rides, trips to town, crab fishing, cinema, picnics, etc. I even bought a 2-man dome tent so we could on little camping trips together by the coast.

Euro Disney was a particularly wonderful experience that we had together. Seeing the Castle just took me back to my childhood, I became a child again and with my beautiful son. Jerry was in his element, so much excitement in his belly, like a kid in a candy shop! This weekend was his time, all about him, I had saved for ages so I could take him. We went on so many rides, saw the Disney Imagination Parade, both bellies full of excitement and exhilaration, seeing all the amazing colourful costumes, hearing the music, meeting all the Princesses and other Disney characters, fills my heart with joy just remembering it and with tears in my eyes. I will never forget that time. So many great memories!

I had a four-year relationship with a lovely man called Stuart, eventually moving into a beautiful cottage with him and Jerry. We had 12 chickens, 2 cats, it was such a beautiful place, remote and safe.

Stuart was a kind man, he had a jovial, silly manner about him, bringing out the kid in me. I started to feel happy again.

He bonded well with Jerry, they would often be heard out in the garden playing games and chasing each other, making chuckling noises as Stuart wrestled Jerry to the floor play fighting. Stuart would use the word 'sweep' and Jerry would know he was going to come after him and sweep him onto the floor. As soon as Stuart said the word, Jerry would chuckle and immediately sit on the floor so he couldn't get him. I would listen, smiling as I went about my day, my heart full of happiness and love for the man that made my son laugh again.

Jerry had started to see his father again, but this was sporadic, with him often letting him down. It seemed Ass A's life revolved around women and poor Jerry was at the bottom of his priorities.

Ass A still tried to control, but I had changed, I kept boundaries in place, arranging pick-ups and drop offs outside a pub a few miles from where we were living.

I had found out he had many other children, Jerry enjoyed spending time with some of his siblings when he stayed with his dad, but the visits were intermittent, and it saddened me why his dad didn't think he was worth bothering with.

The relationship with Stuart ended after I found out he was an alcoholic, I asked for him to leave, whilst Jerry and I remained living in the cottage for a year or so.

I was concentrating on bringing up Jerry and my career. I had a couple of

casual flings, one was Alistair, he said he was Italian, we would meet every so often, sharing time together, which at the time, I valued. Contact stopped when he moved up to Manchester.

Funnily though, his friend Matthew did keep in contact by mobile. He had managed to get my number from Alistair, sent me regular texts and soon he took to calling me for chats. His reasons for keeping in touch were he was interested in me, that sometimes he felt lonely and that he felt good when he spoke to me. He lived in Bradford and I in Suffolk. We kept regular contact until one day he asked if he could meet me. I was in too minds, however, something just felt right when I said yes, we made plans for him to get the bus and come and stay at mine. Jerry was going to mums.

I felt safe as he was Alistair's best friend and Alistair always seemed a nice guy, although a bit of a womaniser, well, he

thought he was, but he was crap at it!!

The first day we met, I met him at the bus stop. I was so nervous, but excited at the same time. When he got off the bus, I noticed how attractive he was, even more than the photos he had sent me.

My height, dark silky hair, deep green eyes and a tanned complexion. He was dressed in fitted blue designer jeans and a fitted black top, with a casual black jacket, designer brown leather shoes. He looked dashingly handsome. I remember my heart was racing madly and he spoke my name in his thick accent and took me into his arms.

We had an amazing weekend together. It was chilled and relaxing, spending many hours talking, getting to know each other, kissing and cuddling.

He worked at a factory in Bradford, said he was Greek like Alistair and was here on a students' visa. I was not worried

by this as I know it was not that difficult to apply to live here when from an EU country.

At the end of an awesome weekend, I drove him back to the bus stop, we said our goodbyes, promising to meet up regularly and see what happens.

Matthew and I continued regular phone calls and texts. It was planned he visit again and for Jerry to be picked up and brought to the house to meet him on the last day. The weekend came and it was as lovely as before. We made love and he appeared very attentive of my body, which I enjoyed. He had a great sense of humor, which reminded me how nan and grandad were together, it was comforting remembering that.

Jerry was dropped off and he bundled in the cottage full of the joys of spring. I had spoken to him prior to this so was aware of Matthew being there.

I remember Jerry running into the house saying hi to me and giving me a hug, then he stood up and looked at Matthew standing leaning against the kitchen sideboard. He said hi to Jerry, Jerry quietly responded, looking at him shyly. I suggested we have a game a football outside, Matthew asked Jerry if he can play? Jerry replied, 'sort of' and Matthew walked with Jerry out into the garden chatting to him about how he used to play football a lot when he was younger.

That was the start of a what I thought at the time was a nice friendship.

Matthew continued to visit us, if it was on a weekend and I had Jerry, Matthew enjoyed his company also, we went so many places, like a family.

It felt good, it felt right. He was good with Jerry, they got on well, like he was a big brother to him, and Matthew was also good to me, like a friend and lover.

After several months seeing each other, he confessed he was in love with me as I was with him.

One day, after a long weekend together, I drove Matthew as usual to the bus station to drop him off to get his bus back home to Bradford. I walked with him to the bus stop, we were both struggling saying goodbye to each other.

We held each other and he kissed me goodbye. He went up the steps of the bus, stopping at the top, turning around to look at me, he suddenly mouthed an expletive and came back down the stairs, grabbing hold of me, saying he hates saying goodbye to me.

He then stopped, thought for a moment and said 'why don't we get married, MARRY ME!'. I was gobsmacked and taken aback. But it felt so right, so despite our situation and not knowing how on earth we would sort this all out,

I went with my heart and gasped 'Yes,Yes!'. We both kissed and embraced each other, saying one last goodbye as the bus was about to leave. I waved goodbye to my loved one, sad to say goodbye but excited at the same time for the three of our futures together.

Our news was not received well by quite a few people. My father was angry Matthew did not ask him permission, also that he had never met this man that I was planning to marry. Mum and my stepdad just wanted me to be happy, they had met him, I think they both may have had some reservations but could also see how happy I was at the same time.

My friends were not sure, my manager at the time took me aside, asking me to think seriously before I marry this man, she was having a bad vibe about it all.

Everyone else was happy for us and we started to plan the wedding, well I did. Matthew kind of left it to me, to be

honest.

I never got an engagement ring, he was a factory worker and said he could not afford one, I was sad about it but understood, now though, I just think he could have just got me a cheap one, the thought would have counted rather than nothing at all.

A few weeks after he proposed to me, Matthew sent me an email. He called me, asking me to read it and have a think, that he will understand if I change my mind about him after I have read it.

The email said that he and Alistair were not from Greece and on working visas like they had both told me. They were both Asylum Seekers from Iran, that Matthew was half Iranian and half Italian. That he had been refused entry to the UK as a Refugee and was currently going through appeals for this.

I was devastated and angry at the same time. His excuse for not telling me was that he knew Alistair had lied to me and he did not have the heart to expose his friend, also he was ashamed of his circumstances.

After some time, considering all what he had said, I made contact and we spoke on the phone. I agreed to still marry him and deep inside hoped and prayed all would be ok.

I then had to break it to my family, it did not go down well at first, but they all took Matthew on face value, seeing how happy jerry and I both were, they decided to accept him into the family.

Financially times were difficult for me, I was a single parent and Ass A was not supporting our son at all and had left me in quite a lot of debt when we split up, of which I was still paying off. I worked part-time and once the bills and debts payments were made, there was not much left.

I was also about to move back to Ipswich as my job had changed, it just made sense being in a town, plus easier for Matthew to find work when we got married.

So, wedding plans were basic, a simple Registry Office wedding, and a reception in a pub in town, with a small buffet prepared by a friend of mine.

The day came, it was special. I walked down the aisle with dad by my side. Dad came but said he could not stay as he was about to go on holiday with his new wife, so left after all the wedding photos were done.

The reception went well, a small pub affair, everyone seemed happy. The wedding night, I had booked the bridal suite at a hotel in a seaside town near us.

When we arrived, we were put into a room, not very special, quite basicMatthew was not happy with it, had a moan at me for bad planning, that the music I played from his country after we said our vows was rubbish, and how I had spent most of the reception dancing with my friends! Our first row on our wedding night, I was blown away, I had literally planned everything, all he had had to do was turn up, yet nothing I had done had been good enough.

This was a warning sign to me, I loved this man! Yet again I was not enough, good enough, I had let him down, even though I had put all my heart into it. The happiness I had felt marrying Matthew was now overshadowed with a dark cloud, looming over our marriage, my life. Wondering if I did really know this man deep down?

He proceeded to tell me that no-one messes with him, and he is not having it. How even his friend didn't get away with treating him bad, how he had left their flat door unlocked and someone had stolen his stereo, so Matthew had felt it appropriate to kick his friend onto the floor as a punishment for letting him down. Matthew said it all with a look of pride and a smile on his face, was this his way of warning me!?

After an awkward few hours, Matthew brightened up, took on the role of consummating our marriage in the way he wished; coldly and without feeling. We then we went out for dinner. We had a lovely walk around the town and along the beach, then back to our hotel to sleep. That weekend, I had paid for everything as he had not got the finances. He never thanked me or showed gratitude for this. It was an expectation and to him, he felt it was my duty to do so.

The next day, I awoke so happy! I was now a wife and felt loved, Jerry now had a stepdad who I thought loved him. I had a little family and was so contented thinking about it all.

We had planned to go to the Home Office to inform them of our marriage, I looked forward to doing this and was positive things would be good for us. We could not have been so so wrong.

The Home Office worker took our details, then said the marriage will not change a thing, that Matthew has been refused entry, if he wishes to live here as my spouse, he must return to Iran and apply for that from there. Matthew tried to explain he cannot, that his life may be at risk if he did so due to his reasons for having to leave his country, the worker reiterated the procedure, saying Matthew needs to speak to his Solicitor re his Asylum Appeal and bid us on our way.

We drove back home in silence, shocked. I was terrified that I was at risk of losing the man I loved, my dear son's step daddy. We got home and slowly went about living our lives, spending a few more days together then I returned to work.

Matthew was unable to work, no NI Number and no Work Visa so financially it was all on me.

I recall my first day back at work. The day was good, I was ok, on my way home, I was in two minds, don't know why, just felt odd. As I drove into the road we lived, I pulled up outside our home. I could see Matthew standing leaning, looking out of the lounge window, in just his white pants, like he was waiting for me.

I suddenly felt pressured, overwhelmed, everything was on me, and I did not like how I was feeling! He came to the door and awaited me, welcoming me and closing the door behind me. It all felt weird.

Financially, things got harder. As I was now living with Matthew, I lost some of my Tax Credits. So I was on a tight budget, had a set amount to spend on things each week, but Matthew did not accept that.

He would often have lots of friends over, treat them like kings, using our weekly food lavishing them with a banquet, then get furious when I tried to explain how we could not afford living like this.

I had had to end Jerry's after school club as could no longer afford it. Matthew would say how he is my slave, that he works for free looking after my son, so he deserves decent food for him and his mates.

He would complain I would not buy him a box of cigarettes each day, it was not a choice, I just did not have the money for it! He would say how I starve him, that it is neglect how I only leave basic food for him when I gallivant off to work. Nothing I did was good enough, it seemed.

We soon got an appointment to see Matthew's solicitor in Bradford. Sadly, the news was the same as what Home Office told us, he advised Matthew to appeal his refusal re Asylum Status and if that is declined, he may have to return to Iran to apply to live here as my spouse. That he was at risk of being deported at any time. We again drove home in silence. I was devastated.

We got home, things went back to as normal as it could be, but I was low, so low. Scared, terrified I may lose my husband. I became depressed, withdrew into myself, we still had not even opened our wedding gifts. The media heard of our plight and came and interviewed us for an article, Matthew told his story, something we both agreed on and felt may help educate people on the plight Asylum Seekers have.

Our lives continued and we did our best to keep going, being as happy as wecould but always with the fear of Matthew being deported at the back of our minds.

Jerry was happily going through life; weekdays at school, evenings with us as a family; dining together, playing silly games and having a lot of fun and laughter.

School holidays and weekends I was working, Jerry and Matthew would go out; swimming, exploring the countryside, going to the cinema etc. I felt happy going to work, knowing Jerry was with Matthew, a father figure I thought he got on well with; it was reassuring.

My depression slowly got worse, I was not making Matthew happy, I was getting more and more into debt and terrified every time the door went, worried it may be Home Office coming to take Matthew away.

Matthew was demanding of me, my attention. Jerry and I were close, enjoying spending time together, we tried to include Matthew, but somehow, he appeared jealous? Wanting me to myself.

He had befriended Jerry, they continued

to do a lot together when I was at work, but Matthew believed when a couple are together, the child takes a back seat, that the woman should put her man first. That was not me.

Sometimes he would ask who I loved the most, him or Jerry? My answer would be 'the love a mother has for her son is different for a wife to her husband, I love you both.'

His demands of me were 24/7. I would work all day and on return, he would expect dinner cooked, house cleaned, I did everything, and I was exhausted.

Then once Jerry went to bed, I was expected to be his entertainment. Socially and sexually. He would demand we stay up late, watch movies, drink, every night. I could not afford this lifestyle he demanded of me, nor did I have the energy, but he would not listen.

Then we would go to bed, it was early hours of the morning by then, I was due to be up for work in several hours. I would get into bed, he would too, then turn around and start on me. Touching, groping, pulling me about, then finishing with anal sex, no lube, no gentleness, in fact it was like he got a rise out of hurting me.

One time, I tried to stop him, explaining how exhausted I was, he ignored me and continued, I allowed it but did not respond, just lying there, tears rolling down my cheeks. A few days later, he woke me, standing over me, shouting in my face, calling me a 'dirty slut, whore, filthy bitch!' as I obviously was seeing someone else, not wanting him. I was not in a great mood, told him it's rubbish, that I love him but to please stop and let me sleep. That was he first time he hit me, a slap in my face. The first time of what was to be many.

The emotional and physical abuse progressed, to most days. He would punish me by the way I looked, if I made a face he did not like, how I behaved in front of others, if I cooked a meal badly, if the house did not look good enough, if I was a 'no good wife!'. Being shouted at, sworn at, laughed at, put down in front of visitors, pushing me, goading me, slapping, pinching, spitting at me, hitting me, punching me.

The demands of sex continued, I learnt to accept and allow it. If I put up a fuss, he would only hurt me more, so I had to let him, force himself upon me, making me bleed, cry, sob, it only egged him further.

I was terrified of him. Jerry did not see much of this initially, but he must have heard, and I hated myself for that.

Yet I was scared to leave, frightened of him. Being honest with myself, the domestic violence started the day I married him, although the grooming was visible prior to this.

At first, it was emotional and verbal, examples being; getting angry and saying I am useless if the dinner I had prepared had gone wrong, swearing at me and calling me degrading words if a man smiled at me if we were out, saying I was a bad mum when I felt unwell with my mental health, some of the terms he called at me regularly were 'psycho', 'freak' 'nutter' etc.

The abuse progressed further from emotional and sexual to financial and physical. He had started to demand money in payment for looking after Jerry after school, even though I was supporting Matthew, that was not good enough. I had no money by the time I paid him, had to resort to buying reduced food and second-hand clothes when Jerry grew out of things.

Matthew watched my every move, if we went anywhere, he would watch how I behave, if I 'misbehaved', I would get it when I got home. If a man smiled at me, it would be my fault, I would be called 'a dirty whore' for apparently encouraging him.

He would even take to embarrassing me in public, once pouring a pint of beer over my head in a pub, all because a man I used to work with said hello. Pushing me about in front of people, he started to become more brave, not even caring what people thought of him.

If meals were not up to his expectations, he would throw his plate of food at the kitchen wall and scream 'no good bitch!'. I was constantly on edge, walking on eggshells.

It only got more dangerous, he started to hit out at my things, and at our home. Sometimes, if he was angry whilst driving, he would stop the car and get out. He would then proceed to kick my car, whilst swearing and shouting, Jerry and I would be inside, frozen in terror, it was so scary.

He seemed to relish that people would hear and stand watching, I felt so embarrassed and ashamed. I would then have to lie and make excuses for the dents in my car, to family and friends that noticed, it was difficult however as one dent was boot shaped.

Now he would take to hitting me, slapping me, kicking me, trying to strangle me, it just kept getting worse in momentum and more and more dangerous.

I stayed as I think I felt, as I have mental health and low confidence, he was all I deserved and I think in my heart of hearts, I thought LOVE would be enough and he would change. He had brain washed me, making me think I was worthless and wouldn't be able to cope without him.

Once holding me by my throat against the wall and trying to strangle me as I was late home from work. Another time, I had dropped Jerry off horse riding,

Matthew had come in the car also. We went for a drive as Jerry was having his lesson. Matthew started to say how we needed to cut money and Jerry's lessons needed to stop. I explained that horse riding is good for him and that I can afford to pay for the lessons. Matthew started to roar and swear, I was still driving at this point.

He proceeded to punch at me as I drove, hitting my face and neck. I pulled in at a local garden centre, hoping someone would see and come and help me, or that Matthew would stop in case someone saw him, he was all about his image you see, Mr Nice Guy! He continued to punch me, repeatedly until he finally calmed down.

I remember going to collect Jerry and having to lie about why my face was red, I was at this point, numb, in shock and completely controlled by this evil man.

After this, I submitted and did everything Matthew demanded, just to keep Jerry and myself safe.

I stayed because I was terrified to leave. He would call me 'psycho, no good mum ' etc. He made me believe it was my fault, I was at breaking point, my mental health had deteriorated. He warned me if I ever left him, he would find me and take it out on Jerry, and I wouldn't want that would I, he would say.

I am no fool, I work as a professional in my job and I have a brain. I think it is only when you suffer Domestic Violence yourself can you truly understand that leaving is not as easy and simple as it sounds.

There were lots of reasons I didn't leave:

- He brain washed me, had near enough taken over my mind; I felt i could not be without him, I was under his control and terrified what he would do to me.

- Due to his treatment of me, my mental health got worse, some of the time, I was so unwell, I couldn't even think straight.

- He said he would kill me and Jerry if I left.

- He had isolated me from my family and friends, I also felt so ashamed, I didn't know where to turn to.

- Sad as it is to say, I loved him.

Matthew told me one day that he wanted to apply to the Iranian Government for a pardon, so he can then return to his country and apply to enter England as my spouse. He made me get a large loan to finance all of this.

He eventually got his pardon and accepted to return to the UK as my spouse. On return, he just got worse. He could now work, had gone to work for my father, who was training him to be a HV Technician.

Now he had money, he got cocky and big headed. He would demand he had half of my money, even benefits and CSA for Jerry.

When we went shopping, he would make me pay myself for anything for Jerry, even though he was pocketing a lot of the money for him. He even had half of my student loan for university. I just got more and more into debt as he got only richer and richer.

I suffered two mental breakdowns whilst I was with Matthew. He had broken me down emotionally, I felt useless and worthless. I also felt I was a terrible mum, putting my poor son through this and Matthew would only reinforce how I felt.

When I felt low, I would withdraw into myself, sometimes cry. He would laugh and encourage me to kill myself, that it would be best for everyone.

Once I took an overdose, I grabbed what tablets I could find and swallowed them.

Matthew knew I did it, yet didn't call anyone, he just watched me, smiling. I was sick so that attempt did not work.

Another time, I felt so low, I looked at my son and hated myself. I knew he often heard and sometimes saw the abuse I was suffering, I felt so guilty, so much blame.

What kind of mother put her son through this?! I am worthless and I felt it would be best for Jerry if I was not here. So, I calmly took my car keys and left the house, planning to drive into a brick wall at high speed. Intent on ending my life.

Only my mobile kept ringing and ringing, I ignored it, determined to finally do the deed and end it all forever! The phone pinged. I had stopped near the wall.

Something told me to look at my mobile, it was a text from poor Jerry 'mum, I love you, please come home! xxxx'. I sat there and I hit reality, and I sobbed and sobbed, tears rolling down my cheeks.

My child saved my life, he was and still is my angel. I took the drive back to reality, terrified what my reception would be. When I finally got home, Matthew muttered 'you should have done it, better for us all!! Crazy Bitch!!!' He then said loudly 'go in there and sit down!', pointing to the lounge, he said he had called my family and apparently, they were on their way. He made Jerry stay upstairs, saying no child should see his mother looking so disgusting as I did right now. I fell onto the sofa and sobbed quietly, not wanting Matthew to hear and anger him further.

After what seemed like ages, the door went, and I heard muffled voices and footsteps. They all went into the kitchen, I was alone, no-one checked I was ok.

My heart was racing as I heard excited murmurs, things I couldn't hear but knew it was about me. I heard footsteps come down the stairs, then heard Jerry crying as a female voice was soothing him.

I said loudly ' I want to see my son, please someone!'. Matthew retorted 'she is NOT safe; he should not see her like this!'. 'But he is my son, I just need to know he is ok, say sorry, cuddle him, please please!!'. I started to sob uncontrollably. My cries were not heard, was to deaf ears as Matthew had the limelight, I have no worth. 'She needs to go in, I am not helping her anymore, none of us can help her. She is too dangerous now, to herself and others. She must go in!'

Matthew persisted into talking my family to taking me to a psychiatric unit to get me help and have me sectioned under the Mental Health Act. 'Please someone please let me see Jerry!'. My family came in to see me, explaining that right now it is best Jerry does not see me like this, that I am not well and need to go to hospital to get some help. I begged and begged to at least say bye to my son and reassure him, only to hear 'she is NOT seeing him!

Look what she has done to the boy? Social Services will take him, she does not deserve her son in this state!'.

My sister agreed to take care of Jerry and my father took me outside to his car. As I am led to his car, I cry out 'Please let me say bye to him dad, please!!' Dad said, 'it will be a while till you can see him love, you need to work on getting yourself better.' He got me into the car and drove me to a local Psychiatric Unit. I cried and cried, calling Jerry's name, I feel my heart is being ripped apart the further and further away from Jerry we drive.

He is gone, I have gone. I am empty now, I have nothing. I am in a dark cloud, trapped, empty, non-existent, worthless, destroyed, torn, void, NOTHING!

I cannot recall how long I was in hospital for, I was a Voluntary Patient and I think it was about 2 months.

Whilst I was in there, I kept a diary, as advised by a Mental Health Worker there.

I shall include some parts of the diary in this section, as and when I feel it appropriate.

All I could think about when I was in there was my family, their faces, how much I had hurt them, especially Jerry. His face when he saw me so unwell, the sound of his crying as I was taken away.

Matthew had given me the added pressure of telling staff and myself that this is something I have to do, that he has had enough and is not prepared to help me, that our marriage is at the brink of breakdown and me getting better is all that will stop this from happening. He also said he questioned my state as a mother right now and whether I am safe to be a parent. I was so scared, terrified of losing my husband and of having my dear son taken away from me for good.

At first, I was put into an Assessment Unit. I was low, anxious, terrified and just felt helpless. Nothing I seemed to do appeared to please my husband, I was now beaten down emotionally and physically, I felt useless as a mum and a wife. No good to anybody. He had taken all the life out of me.

Anyway, dad drove me to the hospital and walked with me to the ward. The nurse in charge signed me in, took my bag and showed me to my room. Dad said bye and left, looking sad and torn walking away. I sobbed, feeling so afraid and alone.

'I feel so so frightened! I am so close now to complete loss of control of my mind, soon I fear I will lose it and die. I will lose Jerry and Matthew if I die, maybe it will be easier on them if I did? I do not want to die though. Part of me wanted to stay, to get stronger and be better so I can be the mum I long to be.'

I do not recall much of the first evening in there, I was made a hot drink, given a handful of tablets and then slept.

I awoke scared, low. Forgetting for a moment where I was. Remembering the night before, driving my car at speed, losing control of my emotions, wanting to die, of no worth on this earth. My intent to drive into a brick wall and how my amazing son saw my intention and sent me that life-saving text. Thinking about how that must have made him feel, I felt wracked with guilt!

I spent most of the day in my room, laying on my bed, ruminating. At lunch, a nurse encouraged me to come into the dining area to eat with the other residents, I did so reluctantly and was surprised to see some people up the table, who looked just like anyone else, without any issues and living their lives. But then when they looked up at me, I saw their eyes. As a young child, I appeared to have the ability to feel others' pain, so when I looked back at these residents, I saw their eyes and into their soles; lifeless, dull, put out, given up, weak, crying out for help.

I sat down next to 2 girls who both smiled and introduced themselves.

After lunch, one asked if I would like to watch a movie with them, it was nice to be offered so I accepted, but not really wishing to, but it's better than lying on my bed alone, right?

As we were watching it, one of them told us how she felt nervous around a male resident. That last night, he had exposed his genitals to her, and when she informed staff, they did not do anything, she felt no-one had believed her. I spoke to a carer, and she said not to worry about it, again like it was a fuss over nothing. It was as if our mental health issues were making it all up, no-one believed us! Yet for this forlorn and anxious woman, it was real.

Later, he came into the day area, looked at us, laughed and gestured with his hips, swaying them provocatively and cupping his crotch. I informed the charge nurse

, who was sitting up the table reading a paper, he looked up at me, sighed and stated he had known this man for many years, that he was likely just playing and returned to his newspaper. We returned to the film, all feeling unsettled and helpless.

Shortly after, I felt thirsty so got up to make a drink, I offered all the other residents one. The male resident came into the room, smiled at me, and asked for a cup of tea.

As I was busying myself preparing the drinks, I failed to notice that he had walked slowly but confidently over and was standing behind me. I froze as I felt a hand settle onto my shoulder and the other on my other one. I asked him not to touch me, terrified what would happen next. He ignored my protest, instead sliding a hand down inside my robe and settled on top of my breast. He held it firmly. I felt sick, panic, jumping

]forward and shouted, 'help me someone!' He pulled his hand away and stepped back, just in time for when the charge nurse raised his head over the top of his paper, saying 'what's up?' with a cannot be bothered attitude. After I told him what happened, a female nurse heard the noise and came to assist. I was listened to, then encouraged to take a tablet and go and lie down. No-one addressed what happened or reassured me, I returned to my room feeling helpless and dirty, vulnerable, and scared, in a unit that was meant to help me get better, where I should feel safe and protected but instead felt violated and uncared for, not important, a woman who was obviously unwell and making up these stories, unbelieved.

Sadly, that night, he entered another female resident's room and sexually assaulted her; that was when they finally listened, he was moved to a more secure unit and the victim sedated. It was like nobody cared, sedate us to keep us quiet?! To make their shift easier, us easier to manage, more pliable.

After that happened, I withdrew more into myself, trusting none of the staff. I felt nauseous thinking about what he did to us all and how it could have been prevented and instead there were now some very unwell and traumatised women. I felt dirty, what happened reminded me of past experiences with men, only to increase my lack of worth to myself and others.

What did happen was the incident brought all the girls closer, we didn't talk about happened but there was an unspoken agreement and understanding. We held each other when we cried, sisters united silently but there for each other.

 As for the staff, the incident was never mentioned again and ward life returned to normal, sedentary, uncaring, minimal effort put in, a sad and melancholy

place, dark and cold, a place where we were alive but not living.

The next day I awoke so low, in such a dark place, black does not even cover it, darker than any colour, in an abyss of emotions but unable to release them. It was as if his hand was still there, I could feel it. It remained there for a long time, I tried to remove it, scratching, tearing at the skin, making myself bleed, yet only sedation calmed me down. I spent the next few days in bed, just existing, breathing drinking and eating, nothing else.

My consultant visited me, a middle-aged woman with long brown hair and round glasses, dressed in a conservative outfit, and a smile of genuine intention.

We spoke about what happened and she listened. I told her how dirty I felt and how the hand is still on my breast touching me.

How my head was permanently buzzing,

I heard voices, telling me I am useless, no worth, unwanted, unloved, that I am a freak and should just do what everyone else wanted and kill myself. My head replayed all the awful things people had said to me over the years, jabbing at me, piercing into my heart, stabbing me with hurtful words and accusations.

I told her how I felt I had no control, that if I get left, I will kill myself, that only the tablets help me. I told her how I was going to die, all the ideas I had. She sat and listened, quietly. She then said how she does not feel I am ready to go home yet, how I need to stay a while until the new medication I am on works. She said she would arrange for me to be moved to a permanent ward, left me advising I rest and try and be good to myself.

That afternoon, I decided to go for a walk out of the unit. I longed to be outdoors, feel the natural air, hear the birds, see the beautiful colors of the outside world.

I have always felt a connection with trees, grass, earth, they all seem to send me love, refresh, ground, reassure and comfort me. I walked and opened my body to the beauty of our Earth, the sounds, smells, sights, feeling the cool breeze against my face, all of my senses being stimulated by the beauty surrounding me. It felt amazing, I felt special, important, beautiful, loved.

For a short moment, I forgot my troubles and became part of nature, Mother Earth giving me the biggest hug and love that I needed, I smiled to myself as I felt her with me, by my side, sometimes even carrying me.

Later Matthew turned up, reluctantly, playing the dutiful husband but not wanting to be there. He was sharp and withdrawn towards me, no love shown.

He demanded I give him my bank card as bills needed to be paid. I tried to explain I do not have much money as I am on sick pay, suggesting maybe he can help this month? He sat staring at me, laughing retorting under his breath so I could hear but no one else in the ward; 'Ha I don't think so, I should charge you for putting up with you, you crazy bitch! Now give me the card woman!'.

Not long after, he left, I sat in the day room. I didn't want to talk to anyone, but I felt safer being around people. I felt lost, unloved, trapped in a relationship that I was too scared to leave. I remember sitting there, rocking slightly, in my own world, too unwell to care anymore or even notice what was going on around me.

It was a quiet evening; most people were watching a film on tv. I recall a new patient entering the room, she looked terrified, was moaning to herself and rocking, she then started to scream and hitting at herself in the face. Staff came running in and they had to restrain her.

I found it deeply disturbing, seeing her fall, hearing her cry, scream and struggle. Seeing the blood from where she had hurt herself. I wanted to get away but was not allowed out at this point as had not long been admitted.

The nearest place to escape was the kitchen, a nurse asked what I was doing, I said making a cup of tea (I hate tea). I closed the door, put on the kettle and took out a mug, standing there motionless staring at the mug. The nurse was suspicious, opened the door, sternly repeating 'What are you doing?' She was so quick, it jumped me out of my state of pondering and shock, causing me to drop the mug, it broke into pieces. I looked down and grabbed the biggest sharpest looking piece and proceeded to cut my wrist, completely oblivious to the nurse being there.

How did the first time feel cutting myself feel? Painful, stinging, yet comforting at the same time. I felt an air of calm over me, but this did not last long! The nurse soon broke me out of my calm feeling, chastising me for what I did, telling me if I continue to break things, I will be reported to the police for criminal damage! I just stared at her in disbelief, is that what they get taught to say when someone has self-injured? ! Another nurse took me to the clinical room and tended to my wounds.

The next afternoon, the residents were planning a take-away and film. The nurse on duty said for me not to worry about ordering anything as it was likely I shall be discharged shortly. I asked why and repeated what the Consultant had told me. The nurse said I am not mentally unwell at all and just need to go home and rest. That they cannot help me, they have seen improvements and I appear more relaxed now. I probably was, but only because I was heavily sedated, the thoughts were still there! I became distraught and anxious, crying begging him not to release me, that I will die, he replied I cannot put that on them, it is my decision if I choose to kill myself or not. The nurse walked away leaving me inconsolable with my new friends, my sisters, comforting me.

Later the charge nurse came in, saying there had been a mistake, they had spoken to my Consultant, that I was going to be moved to a permanent ward after all and was staying.

I felt so much relief, was found a bed and moved into Mistley Ward. The staff greeted me with a welcoming smile and helped me unpack. I felt safe, wanted, welcomed. Yet why did the unit treat me like this, why did they make me feel such an unwanted nuisance, and why did they trigger me, saying what they did?!

I later found out the unit was due to close, the staff being made redundant, it appeared obvious after hearing this,

that they had stopped caring, given up.

Sadly, just before I was admitted into hospital, my dear nan had passed away. Mum was trying to deal with her mum's death but also deal with the fact her youngest daughter was in a Psychiatric Unit, a lot to have to cope with.

Mum informed my sister of the plans for the funeral, and she came and saw me to tell me. Plans were made for myself to go with my sister, stay the night before at my Aunties. Matthew would bring Jerry in our car and meet us there. The ward agreed for me to do this and return the next day.

I was collected by my sister, and we drove to my Aunties, where I took a sedative and went to bed.

The next day was the funeral. It is all a blur, I was so sedated, I did not feel any emotions and struggled to keep my eyes open.

I got dressed and my sister did my hair, we then made our way to nan and grandads. I recall my grandad giving me the biggest hug. Putting his big arms around me, crying quietly as he did so.

My sister went outside to answer her phone, to come back not long after, informing me my car had blown up on the A14, that they were ok, but Matthew and Jerry would be late.

The funeral started and I sat alone. I don't know why but I felt alone, like no one else was there. I was very anxious as I knew how stressed Matthew would be and likely to blame me for it all. When the vicar spoke, he spoke about nan and the family, it appeared everyone but me was mentioned, it maybe I missed my name. I was so drugged up.

After the funeral we went back to nan and grandads, Matthew and Jerry were there, I gave Jerry the biggest hug, holding him in my arms, so happy to see him and hold him again. As I did so, I felt Matthew's eyes burn into me angrily. He did not need to say anything and would never do it in front of people, the impeccable charmer. His eyes said it all. I kept out of his way.

I returned to the ward that evening, tired and weak from such a long day.

The next day, I got myself up and decided to put my all into getting better. I signed up for all the activities in the ward. My Key Nurse sat with me and asked my intentions for getting better. My answer was to get my son back, be a good mum and leave my husband. I had started to realise the main cause for my emotional fall was Matthew, all the abuse had broken me. I needed to recover and get my strength back so I can leave him, start my life afresh with my boy.

The worst part about being in hospital was not seeing Jerry. So, it made my day when dad called, saying that he was picking him up, that we were going to go to the park the 3 of us. I made a huge effort that morning to look nice. A nurse helped me. When I saw Jerry, he looked so pale and tired. He smiled and ran to me for a hug, I choked back tears, trying to stay brave for him.

We had a picnic and Jerry played in the play area; it was lovely. When the time came for me to go back to hospital, my heart sank. Saying goodbye was extremely difficult, Jerry looked sad as I waved bye, it broke my heart and filled my body with guilt and shame.

This day made me realise what I had to lose but also what I had to gain. My son was my everything and he needed me more than ever. felt I had failed him by my wrong choice in men and by becoming unwell like this.

Things had to change and fast! On return to the ward, I spoke to my key nurse again, asking for all the help I can get to recover, so I can go home to be with my son. We discussed why I was in a rush to leave; I explained my relationship with Matthew, the first time I had told anyone.

She sat silently listening. At the end, she asked if I realised it was not my fault, that Matthew is committing Domestic Violence and abuse. Being brainwashed and abused so long, I had not even thought about it being dv, he had battered me so much emotionally and physically for so long, I didn't really have the ability to have my own mind. I was like a robot, I had submitted to full control by him, for the safety of my son and myself.

Her saying that to me without him being there to defend himself meant it made me ponder. She explained the reasoning for her comment, asked me more questions, of which I safely feel I could open up more and more.

By the end of the conversation, it was

felt I was a victim of Domestic Violence, all aspects. I felt shocked inside. She offered and made a vow to help me get through this, get better, stronger so I can finally leave this man who I loved so much but also hated at the same time for doing all this to me, when all I had done was try and love him with my whole heart.

My priority now was to recover, get stronger, be able to leave this monster safely and start life again with my beautiful little boy. The thought of us being happy and free filled me with excitement and spurred me on to get there.

There were two sides of me, one who so wanted to leave, be free, no longer have to walk on eggshells every minute of my life, no more being beaten to a physical and emotional pulp, no more feeling scared, being free and seeing my son happy again! Yet, I still bloody loved this evil man and deep down I wished that everything would be all right, he would see the error in his ways and change. But I was dreaming the impossible, yet not well enough to realise this.

Despite these feelings, I knew if I didn't make the changes needed, I could be at risk of losing my son, something I was not prepared to have happen. It was an easy to decision to make when I thought about it like that.

I continued to work hard on my recovery, my goal to be with Jerry again and try and make it up to him for being unwell and being such a terrible mum. I saw a psychiatrist weekly, joined a therapy group, an art group where we had an artist come in and teach us art, I found it really helped me ground, also a way to express myself safely in my artwork.

I joined the gym, started going there, went out for walks, generally took the offer up of most of the services in the hospital.

I did everything I could and engaged with anyone who could help me. Determination and strength filled my body, I was going to do this!

Sometime after, a meeting was called and it was decided I would be part-time discharged and become an Outpatient, it meant I was allowed back home, but had to attend the hospital in the daytime. Matthew reluctantly agreed (had no choice really did he!?) and I made the plans to come home.

Initially, I stayed with a friend who took care of me, excitedly collecting my son from my sisters who allowed him back to me, somewhat reluctantly. Things started to look better for us and I started to make plans.

I went to the Suffolk Council, spoke to them re my housing situation, who confirmed if Matthew left, I would get some Housing Benefit to assist me in paying my rent.

I spoke to Women's Aid on the phone who gave me support and advice re Safety Planning. I started to see light, a future without Matthew. Part of me was so sad about this, our marriage down the drain like this. Not what I had planned for at all. I felt a failure but knew I had to, at some point leave. Not just for me but for Jerry.

One evening, Jerry and I were having tea together as Matthew was working late. Jerry asked if he could tell me something. I said of course. He proceeded to tell me that he was very frightened I may die. That maybe I will kill myself or Matthew might harm me. That he is scared that if something else goes wrong or someone upsets me, I might decide to finally end my life. That he would be alone and who would look after him? My heart broke and I cried inside, screamed even. Yet I kept my composure and reassured him I had no intention of doing that, that I truly love him, won't be leaving him.

He shed a tear or two and came and wrapped his little arms round me. That night took away any second thoughts of my needing to leave Matthew, it was only now a matter of when the time is right and safe to.

Time flew by, I returned to work, and Jerry went back to school. Matthew was working still and would come home his usual self, King of the Castle, expecting everything to be done for him, to be waited on. I did so, I kept the peace, the marital rape continued but I managed to put on a great act, I spiritually imagined a veil on me protecting me. I just kept going, waiting for the time to come when my son and I can flee.

Easter weekend came up. Jerry and I had started to go to a Pentecostal church, we had been invited to a Good Friday service, which ended with a cooked meal and the option to watch the film The Passion Of Christ.

I explained to Matthew before we left and went to church. I recall saying we would be home after lunch. In the service, I turned my mobile off, my intention of turning it back on when it ended. It was a beautiful service, after we headed to the day area for a lovely cooked Jamaican meal. It was so nice seeing Jerry mixing with his friends, looking so happy and contented.

After the meal, we were asked if we would stay for the film, Jerry begged to be able to, he clung onto me 'please mum please!!' with a huge smile on his face. Well, I couldn't say no to my son's beautiful expectant face, so we stayed. I was so relaxed, I didn't worry that I had not turned my phone back on, this was Jerry and My day! It was a wonderful day, so much love shown to us and a safe place to be.

As we walked back home, I remembered to turn my phone back on and it was then the joy and happiness inside of me was ripped out and replaced with fear and terror. Ping ping ping ping my phone went on and on, missed calls, texts, voicemails, on and on, over and over. The voicemails of Matthew screaming down the phone 'Where are you you crazy bitch?! Get home NOW!' 'We have friends coming for tea, my mates, YOU MUST cook for us, we are waiting, you useless FUCKING BITCH!' 'get back now, I am mad angry, YOU DID Not get permission to stay out this late and believe me, I AM MAD!!!' 'Fucking bitch, wait till you get back!'.

I couldn't listen or read anymore, choosing instead to ignore them, sending him one text, saying I am now on my way home. All the way back, the phone rang on and off, ping ping ping. Jerry had heard the shouting voicemails. He said 'Mum, please mum, can we leave now? Matthew is too angry, we are not happy, he makes you unwell. PLEASE MUM

PLEASE! I do not like this anymore.' I agreed we will leave and I returned home with Jerry, not thinking straight, just wanting to get back and get some things, go to a friend's just for the night till I decided what to do.

When we arrived, I asked Jerry to go up to his room, I reassured him all would be ok, he did so and quietly closed his room.

Matthew was waiting in the lounge, he stood up saying 'WELL!!???' I said nothing, he shouted 'YOU FUCKING BITCH! WHO do you think you are? I DID NOT give you permission to be out all day! PLUS my friends were here, we waited hours for food to be prepared for us as a GOOD WIFE would do! YOU NO GOOD fucking bitch of a wife. YOU do Nothing for me, cannot even please me in bed! NO wonder I go elsewhere!'

I calmly explained we were at the church all day as he knew. He replied 'YOU are late woman!! AND you didn't get my permission to stay out! Where is my dinner ey ey?!' I suggested he get himself something. 'I am warning you, you are pushing me to end it, should I leave, is that what you want!?' thinking I would get upset and beg him not to.

It was then I told him I think I cannot make him happy or give him what I want, and yes it may be a good idea if he did leave, maybe stay at a mates till we decide what to do with the house? He stood at stared at me coldly, 'is that what you want? You have used me and now want to throw me into the gutter? WELL my dear, I aint going nowhere, YOU and your spoilt brat black child can leave!' I then reminded him that how when we first moved in together, he had agreed if we ended, that he would leave as I have Jerry.

I asked him politely and respectfully if he would please mind going to stay at a friends for the night and then we can talk

 about how we will end our marriage etc, the practicalities etc.

He stood staring at me coldly, I looked back and said 'I will give you space to get some of your things, I will go and sit with Jerry upstairs.' I left the room and went up the stairs into Jerrys' room who was on his PlayStation, sat beside him, reassuring him that Matthew will be leaving soon.

Little did I realise that Matthew was downstairs winding himself up, his anger rising to boiling point. I heard him come upstairs and walk into our bedroom. Assuming he was there to pack, I proceeded to chat to Jerry about the game he was playing.

All of a sudden, I heard Matthew run back downstairs shouting, more like roaring 'YOU FUCKING USELESS BITCH. IF I CANNOT HAVE OUR HOME, MY HOME then neither can you!!' I heard him opening and closing drawers,

I quickly got Jerry to get up and come into the bathroom so we could lock ourselves in safely, my heart was pounding. I heard glass smashing and him laughing excitedly as he was smashing the downstairs windows of the house, shouting obscenities as he did so.

As I locked the door, I could hear Matthew running up the stairs, roaring like a wild beast, 'I will FUCKING have you you bitch!' He tried the door, yelling at me to open it and let him in. I explained calmly not until he calms down, then we can talk, but not with Jerry here. 'You do not tell ME what to do! How dare you!'.

I heard crashing on the door, more and more knocking, banging, crashing, then his hand came through it, then his whole self and the door was crashed through. He tried to get at Jerry but I just laid myself over him.

He hit at me with what looked like a

hammer, but I used my arms to shield myself. Somehow, with a lot of pushing and shoving, Jerry and I got out of that room, I yelled at Jerry to run as I took his hand and we started to run down the stairs. At one point I tripped and regained my posture to continue, Matthew reached us, he lunged for us both with the hammer (a claw hammer) raised in his hand, roaring loudly.

I recall Jerry slowing down and looking behind him, hearing him say calmly but loudly 'No Matthew please, let us leave.' And we proceeded to continue down the stairs and out of the house.

We ran to the neighbors who were standing outside their house, having heard the ruckus, they informed me they had called the police and stood with me till the police arrived.

Matthew was a coward, he did not come outside, not until the police arrived and made him leave, by arresting him and putting handcuffs on him.

I stayed with my neighbors till the police had taken him away. The rest is a blur, of panicking, crying and just trying so hard to keep it together for my son.

Some of my church mates arrived and the men temporarily repaired the broken windows. The police spoke to me and took the information they needed; they did not speak to Jerry. (Later a year or so after this, Jerry informed me how Matthew had tried to hit at my head with the claw of the hammer and that was why he had slowed down on the stairs, that he had stood behind me to protect me and asked Matthew to stop and allow us to leave. How sad the police did not speak to him as I feel he would have not got away with what he did so much if they had known all that)

After the windows were made safe, we were allowed to return, the police said he would be in overnight and it released tomorrow, he will be advised not to return to the house alone, that he can come if someone attends with him to help him collect his belongings and with prior arrangement with myself.

Jerry and I returned to the house, spending the night there but neither of us sleeping much.

Family came and supported us. Matthew was released with a Caution, and he arranged to collect his belongings with a friend present. My brother-in-law remained there whilst they did so, to ensure he only took what was his.

A month or so after that, my sister convinced me to move in with her and apply for homelessness, with the view to moving in the same village as her. We agreed and Jerry and I moved there. It took several months and then we were offered a Council House near her. Great times ahead or so I thought!

We bought two little puppies called Matilda and Poppy, beautiful little things, one each ! Jerry had Poppy but loved them both the same, it was a way for him to get love and affection, he was soon devoted to these dogs.

All was well initially, but sadly, we lived there only for short period, due to issues with my sister, our relationship broke down. I applied for a Council House swap and, after a few viewings, Jerry and I found a beautiful little house in a very quiet, peaceful village, with a huge garden.

In fact, Jerry asked if we could live there as soon as he saw the back garden and before he even stepped inside the house ! After arrangements were made, we moved and remain living there to this very day.

And now to the rest of my life !

6.

The Disclosure and Court

Hell tempting my heaven

The rushing waterfall

cascading down the mountain

billowing clouds of water and glistening silver droplets

shimmering in the sun

I hear the wind rushing through the trees

trinklets of water hitting the rocks

I smell the mountain dew

I see an opening; a rush of light from above

sunlight streaming through, rays beaming down

a picture of paradise, like heaven to me

Something is hidden deep inside the waterfall

reaching out to me, deadly shapes, sinewy bodies

writhing and grimacing with the flow of the water

I close my eyes, thinking of the peace

trying to shut out the evil visions

As I listen, suddenly, quietly

I hear the voice of an angel

relaxing my state of mind.

We settled well into the new home, the villagers appeared very nice, lots of village activities that we took part in. Such as; badminton, bingo, pub nights etc. We soon happily settled into village life. We both started to feel safe again. Jerry settled into a new school and things seemed to settle for a while.

Everything was ticking along nicely at home, Jerry was settled at school and life felt good.

One day one of my old church friends, Miranda, made contact. She informed me she had seen Matthew, how well he looked, that he was coming to church with his new partner. How in love they were and what a lovely couple. No concerns for how what she was telling me may have made me feel, and complete disregard for what this man had done to me before. I was gobsmacked, just replied 'how nice. Let's hope he doesn't treat her like he did me hey!', she replied 'oh I don't think so, she is a very kind and gentle woman and brings out the best in him.'

After that conversation, I realised some people that I thought were my friends clearly were not and I re-evaluated a few things, one was steering clear of her!

I didn't hear anymore from Miranda for some time. One evening, whilst I was chilling out in my lounge, my mobile rang. It was her, she was very sharp and

blunt, did not even ask how we were.

She proceeded straight in to inform me that Matthew and this woman had sadly ended, that she had had a child with him. There were concerns for Matthew being safe to see his child and his ex was trying to contact me. I agreed with Miranda for her to give her my telephone number. I did have to say something also 'Oh so was he not as kind as you thought then or maybe he just hadn't changed after all as you thought hey!' Miranda said maybe she had been rash in her judgement in it all. I agreed and bid her goodnight. I really had nothing to say to her, she had made herself clear the last time we spoke.

A few nights later my phone rang. It was Matthew's Ex Heidi. She asked if it was ok to talk and then told me about whatwas happening. She had recently ended it with him as he had started to show signs of being a Narcissist and had a temper.

He had not hit her but had started to push her and be controlling of her.

She asked me why I had ended my marriage with him. As Jerry was at home and wandering about being nosey, I asked if I could speak with her another day.

She called back two days later and again, Jerry was home. As I was talking to her, Jerry came into the room. He had overheard me talking with Miranda previously so had some inkling of what was going on. He asked me if it was Matthews's ex, I politely explained to him I am on the phone and will talk to him later. I ended the call with her, and we planned to speak again soon.

That night, Jerry had many questions, why was she in touch, what did she want, why why why?! I explained her circumstances and as soon as he found out Matthew had a child, he said 'he is not safe to see her and should not be

allowed mum, tell her please?!' he appeared anxious.

I asked him if he wanted to talk to me about it, he said no but asked if he can talk to her when she calls again, I explained it would not be good idea but I am happy to tell her what he wants to say. He said no, don't bother mum, quite annoyed and left the room.

I did not hear from Heidi for a few weeks so assumed she had got the resolution she wanted and no longer needed to speak to me. Jerry started to have disturbed sleep and his schoolwork suffered. I was worried about him; I spoke to the school Pastoral Worker who tried to talk to him but Jerry did not want to speak to anyone.

About a month after I last heard from her, Heidi called again. Jerry was upstairs. I decided I just wanted this, so spoke to her and started to answer the questions she had for me.

After a few minutes, Jerry entered the room demanding to speak to her. I explained no and why, but he was very persistent. I asked him why he wanted to, Jerry said he didn't want to tell me, that he wants to talk to her on his own and for me to leave the room. I calmly explained that cannot happen. He got more and more upset and by this point, he was crying and raising his voice. I asked why he was so upset 'Mum you don't get it! Please mum let me talk to her, Matthew can't be near her baby tell her tell her!!!' I explained I have advised her of this but that he cannot speak to her. I reassured him that everything will be ok. 'But mum no one knows he is dangerous mum really, he shouldn't be allowed around children, he is horrible mum! You just don't know. Please tell her tell her he cannot be alone with the baby at all. Please!' He was sobbing with tears running down his cheeks. I was startled, something just wasn't right. I looked at him, he shouted it over and over and Heidi heard. I said to Heidi, I will call her later but needed to go and speak to Jerry. Before we put the phone down Jerry screamed ' no no no mum, don't let her go, no!' I asked him why he was so worried, was there something he wanted to say?

It was then I thought my life was going to end and a part of me died. My son replied 'He cannot see the baby mum, because because he is dangerous mum. Because he he he he hurt me, he used to hurt me when you were at work. Matthew hurt me many times.' He blurted it all out, then left the room running up to his bedroom crying his eyes out. I quickly ended the call with Heidi and went up to Jerry. Jerry refused to talk, said 'it is what it is' was dismissive and said he wished to be alone. I told him I loved him and gave him his space.

The next day, I got Jerry up, saying did he want to take the day off school, he said no and went off on the school bus. I took the day off work and called the Pastoral Worker at Jerry's school, asking for an urgent appointment, meeting her that afternoon.

I informed her what Jerry had said and she said she would spend some time and talk with him. A Safeguarding referral was made, and he was referred to CAF, the Common Assessment Framework. It took some time, but eventually Jerry told her what had happened, and some bits he told me.

Basically, Matthew had taken to beating Jerry for the six years we had been married. I am not going into it in great detail out of respect to my son.

It was agreed we would call the police. They came and they asked to speak to Jerry alone. Jerry looked terrified. When the meeting was over, they informed me

Jerry had decided not to press charges as there is not enough evidence, as it was a few years ago.

I was devastated, Jerry later told me they had explained what would happen re court etc and how Matthew would likely get away with it. I asked him if he would like to speak to a solicitor and see if there is a chance, he agreed. We went, only to be told the same. I am sorry but I wonder if the same would have been said if Jerry had been a girl!?!

Heidi called again several weeks later. She was so kind, worried for Jerry, asking how he was.

She then asked if Jerry would be prepared to say in an Access Court what Matthew did to him? That it may protect her little girl so that he cannot do the same for her.

I spoke to Jerry who agreed to do this. I was so proud of him.

Several months, meetings with her Solicitor and many statements later, Jerry stood up in court telling the judge what this evil man did to him.

I remember being told the judge asked Jerry if he is still scared of him, apparently Jerry replied no, and when the judge asked him why, he stood up and said 'because I am now taller than him!'.

So proud of my boy but also so ashamed at myself for letting my boy down, by not protecting him as a good mother should. That guilt I felt was to breed and grow in me and was the reason for my mental health state of fall later in this book.

I encouraged Jerry to get some counselling and I contacted 4YP, a local charity. He saw someone several times, then told me he didn't wish to go anymore, that he just wants to move on. I respected that, saying if he ever needed to talk, I am there, or we can re re-refer him for support.

We both struggled in our own way and found our own way to deal or not deal with it.

And so, our life settled and continued.

When Jerry was born, I had an intention of taking him to Jamaica when he was old enough so he could see and learn about his dad's side of the family and culture. Every year, I had saved my pennies.

The time came when I had enough money to book the tickets and off we went. Prior to going, I had tried speaking to Ass A, explaining I was taking our son to Jamaica, asking where their family lived, if he could put me in touch with them? He was reluctant, so I said, if not, just the areas so we could go there. He said he would think about it and get back to me, which he never did.

So, we went there with the plan to explore some of the country, especially in areas we knew some of his family were

from. I have to say it was one of the best experiences of my life.

I was not rich by any means but I had saved well for this. The first word we learnt when we got there was 'irie'. (ahy-ree) which is a saying often used to mean 'everything is alreet and fine.'

Well we had a right irie time! Lots of voyages, including; St Elizabeth Falls, Black River safari, Dunns River, Appleton Estate rum distillery, a Boat Trip on the ocean and a Fishing trip on a boat with locals.

Well, so much I could say here about the highlights of our amazing voyages. The boat trip on the ocean brought some fun and laughter, mainly because we were given Life Jackets to wear, only I am large chested, mine was way too small.

When I was being zipped up, I had to lift my breasts up so I could fit in the jacket. The Lifeguard finished zipping me up and smiled when I stood back.

His mate and himself were appraising me and, with their arms folded saying 'irie man!!' I turned round only for Jerry's eyes to nearly pop out of their sockets and said 'the term Betty Boop comes to mind' and everyone laughed. Only then did I look down and notice my breasts had beenpushed right up high and nearly falling out at the top of the life jacket. Oops!

Appleton Estate was another experience. Being given a tour of the distillery, being told that the workers were only allowed to work in the Rum Barrel storage fifteen minutes at a time as the fumes make them drunk. At the end, we were taken to the bar and offered to sample as much as the rum as we wished. Jerry and I decided to start at one end and see how far we got. Well needless to say, we did not get far and poor Jerry had to help me get up the stairs onto the bus as a I was a bit tipsy!

The Black River safari, seeing the crocodiles in the wild, one came up to the boat and Jerry stroked it. He, however, declined the offer to swim with him.

Jerry particularly enjoyed climbing Dunns River and jumping into the spring at the end. Seeing the joy on his face warmed my heart, the best therapy ever is seeing your child happy and to know you helped to do that.

Jamaica was a special time for us both, Jerry reaching some milestones, one being losing his virginity one evening on the beach looking over the star lit ocean as he was being seduced by an older woman.

My curves being a BBW were appreciated by a lot of the Jamaican men. In fact, I unintentionally pulled three men. One, the Restaurant Manager, another was a Lifeguard.

Then there was Beanie Man. Beanie man came and sang at the resort, at the time he was not world famous. At the end, we were all invited to dance on stage, which we did.

Beanie Man and I had a dance, he writhed his sinewy body against mine, me soon realising he had no underwear on under his clothes. He nuzzled into my neck 'Gimme your room number…' he muttered. I quickly denied and soon returned to Jerry. It was only a year or so later, Jerry had MTV on television and said 'mum, look, that man singing is Beanie Man who tried to chat you up in Jamaica'. I'm drinking Rum and Red bull is what I hum to myself when I think about him.

We returned home happy and contented, with a positive outlook on our future.

7.

The end of the road and coming back

If it wasn't for you, I'd be gone by now
· ·

Grounding

Rooting...

finding your way to the motherland

sinking into the Earth, entwining into one

Going...

releasing, letting go, allowing it

feeling the energy, feeling the love, feeling mother's touch

Welcoming...

the release, letting go, sinking deeper

re-joining the earth.

The guilt. To feel the guilt, as a mother, for not protecting my son. It just ate away at me, stripping away, until I could cope no more. I regularly had flashbacks of the trauma I had suffered. When I was awake and in my dreams, so many bad nightmares that I was scared to fall asleep at night.

I continued to work and try and be the best mum I could. With hardly any sleep and running on autopilot but also in a deep depression. Some days, I couldn't do it, I just couldn't face the world, I would stay in bed.

Poor Jerry became my carer on these days, trying to encourage me to get up, wash, dress, everything was a huge chore, I had no interest, motivation, or energy.

These days became more often and soon each day started to roll into one. I soon became the useless mum that Matthew used to say I was. It was like a self-fulfilling prophesy. I was riddled with guilt, for being a bad mum and not protecting my son or keeping him safe from this monster, and then became even more of a bad mum by losing myself yet again to my Mental Health conditions.

I did reach out, I tried to get help. I was under the Community Mental Health Team and seeing a psychiatrist, he said I had PTSD and Cyclothymia. I saw him once a fortnight I think, to talk, and he medicated me.

Many times, I would call the Mental Health Team, feeling suicidal, to be told how well I am doing, because I am so self-aware, and 'why don't you go andmake yourself a nice cup of tea?' or be told 'you are in control, this is not mental health, it is a life choice if you choose to live or die or not. You are not as ill as you feel. We cannot help you, this is down to you!!' None of those comments helped me, in fact they triggered me. PLUS I am allergic to tea!

I started to self-harm, first doing this in my first stay in hospital as mentioned in the previous chapter. I used a razor, on my wrist, initially, but once people started to notice, I started cutting further up my arm. I tried to hide it from Jerry, but he soon started to realise when I quietly went into the bathroom and locked the door, that was what I was going to do.

Him finding out only drove the guilt in me deeper and deeper and reinforced the bad mum I was. Him knowing his mum was cutting herself, how bad was I?! That poor lad had been through enough because of me. Cutting at this time was a release of the emotional pain, the physical pain overrode the emotional pain I was feeling.

But it also started to help me punish myself, 'dig a bit deeper so it hurts, there!serves you right for all the pain you have caused poor little Jerry!' I would say to myself, well more a voice in my head would say to me.

I referred Jerry to a Young Carer organization, for support for him. He started to go to a monthly youth club and had respite breaks, which he really seemed to enjoy.

I had a couple of short stays in hospital, two for passing out, had palpitations, stayed in a general ward, had checks and was discharged, they put the passing out and palpitations as anxiety, but no support or medication was given for it.

My memory is a haze, I recall when I self-injured and a close friend took me to a and e. After hours of waiting, I saw someone, they listened, said I was very selfaware, that they did not believe I was as unwell as I thought I was as I was so self-aware, I told them I did not feel of value to anyone, not even my own son.

That sometimes I felt I should leave this world. They reassured me, said I was doing a good job and sent me on my way! I was dumbfounded but also felt very let down.

Another time, I disassociated and ended up in my car driving, scared as I did not know where I was. I called my sister and spoke to her, later going to hospital again, seeing the Crisis Team, who spoke to me, listened, and again sent me on my way. By this point, I felt helpless, with no-one to turn to.

It got to a point, I was in a living hell, flashbacks, racked with guilt, eating at me. Surges of emotions running through me.

Some days I couldn't get out of bed, wouldn't get dressed or washed. Most times I tried to get up and would go to work. But after nights full of nightmares and lack of sleep, I had no energy, I couldn't wash or anything, I took on the habit to put talc on to disguise the smell, and wear a hat so no one would notice my greasy hair.

I would struggle at work, come home, and be exhausted, trying to act ok is so tiring, I would come home and collapse onto my bed. Jerry again took the role of my carer, prepared tea and just kept encouraging me. I was broken and because of that, yet again a bad mum, the vicious cycle, more and more guilt of being crap as a mum, failing him, getting more and more unwell.

Reading this, you may feel disgusted at me. But I did try, I went to my gp, I spoke to the CMHT, I tried everything to get better, attended all the groups I was advised to attend. But nothing seemed to work and no-one seemed really to want to help me. The guilt of what Jerry suffered ate at me and poisoned me inside, I did not feel worth being on this earth and truly believed that Jerry would be better off without me.

I got to the point I felt on edge 24/7, was not sleeping, constantly anxious and constantly beating myself up as a mother. By this point, nothing anyone said to me helped, as far as I was concerned, I had failed to protect him and keep him safe as any mother should.

It all came to a head one day. I had started attending a Bible Study group with a friend, had made a few friends, or so I thought.

One evening, Jerry came with me and was giving me a lot of attitude towards me in front of the group. I tried to talk to him quietly, asking him to stop, to try and be respectful. Jerry just got worse. I realise now he was likely just being a typical lad showing off in front of some girls he had recently met.

It got a bit confrontational with Jerry stomping out of the church. I found him and we both got into the car and headed home. By the time we got home, he had apologised, and I apologised for getting upset at him in front of his friends.

The next day, I got a message from one of the younger women at the church, telling me I was too stern with Jerry, that he did nothing wrong, that I need to look at myself as a mother, how bad it was to see. I replied, was polite, thanked her for her text and her comments and that Jerry and I were fine now. I wasn't prepared to go into detail as to why we were both struggling a bit. She continued texting, saying I was a terrible mum, that last night I was abusive to him, and she might contact Social Care Services.

By this point, I was triggered. I asked her to please stop messaging me, told her how I am not feeling too good right now and I would like to be left alone.

I tried ignoring her but still the messages came.

I was already living on the edge, sadly this woman was reinforcing what I already thought of myself and what the two main perpetrators of my life had shouted or whispered into my ears over the years. I felt huge emotional pain and anxiety, this woman would not stop, more and more messages, beating me down further further!

I was sobbing, couldn't breathe. I was done, too many times had I heard or read these harsh words, so as far as I was concerned, they must be true! 'I AM A BAD MUM! He would be better without me as all I do is hurt him or bring people into his life that hurt him.' It was then I truly wanted to die, not for me but to release my son from me. I was not worth or deserving to be on this earth so I must go now.

I left my house, got into my car and drove silently, but fast with determination for what must be done. It is my time! I got to my destination, was now on a dual carriageway, I do not recall how I got there as I cried all the way, my eyes glassy with my tears.

I parked my car in a parking layby and sat there in silence. By this point, I had no control over my thoughts, there were no tears left in me, I wiped my face and opened the door, proceeding to get out of the car.

It was a busy time of day; I do not recall what time it was, but I do remember how busy the traffic was. I remember how I ran across the road back and forth waiting to be hit, but that time didn't come, all that happened was cars screeched and hooted. I ran back and forth; I recall feeling a buzz of excitement. I looked at the road surface and thought I could just lay down and then it would happen.

I stepped forward into the road, tried to sit down, feel down, sat up, trying to will myself to lay down, 'don't be so so weak, just do it, lay down woman! Do what is right! Do it do it do it now! Look at you, it is pathetic! You are useless you cannot even kill yourself, look at you!' I stood up and started to scream, I wanted to die so why couldn't I do it? Why am I so weak!?

By this time, someone had pulled over and shouted for me to 'stop please, you will hurt yourself and others! Please come to the side of the road my dear!' I looked over and saw an elderly woman sitting in her car with her head out. I walked to the side of the road as she asked. She asked me to please stay by the side of the road, reassuring me help will be here very soon.

I heard a calmness in the road and when I looked, I saw no more cars were going past this side of the carriageway. Not long after, I saw flashing lights and heard a siren. 2 police cars attended the scene and supported me.

It is all a haze, but I remember how comforting they were, gently spoken, reassuring me, trying to encourage me into one of the police cars which I started to do, then hesitated, looking back at the carriageway one last time, one of the police said 'oh no you do not! Get in the car NOW!'

Giving me a quick shove, I stopped looked at him and then proceeded to shove him back, then I laughed loudly, excitement making me buzz, mania at its peak. He smiled at me and asked me gently to get into the car, that he did not want to force me but that I and members of the public are in danger, so I must get into the car. I stepped back and bent to get in, he quickly took one of my hands and helped me quickly giving me a gentle shove to get me in. So, I fell into the car.

He later apologised for doing that, such a kind and respectful man he was. I was driven to the local hospital and 2 policemen had to sit with me I think for about 5 hours until a nurse eventually arrived, spoke to them and myself then admitted me into the Psychiatric ward under a police section.

I cannot recall how long I was in there, but it was quite a long time. It is all a haze of memories; I do not remember what treatment I had other than I was put on different medication.

The Psychiatric wards had moved onto a general hospital, there were less wards and less services. The nurses seemed busy all the time, but I do not know what they were busy doing as they didn't speak to the patients much. They left us to it and spent most of their time at the nurse's station or chatting together in their office.

There was a room with art equipment, no-one led any classes, but I sometimes went in and did some drawing or painting.

I watched lots of tv, well sat in front of the tv, staring into space more like. Not many other patients spoke to me, we were all mostly in our own worlds. Every day seemed the same, one rolled into another.

Then, one day, I was called to a Meeting and this nice man, Pierre attended. He introduced himself to me, saying that when I am discharged, he will be my Care Co-ordinator. The Consultant said I was doing well and responding well to my new medication, I was diagnosed PTSD and BPD. Discharge was set and two weeks later, I was back home.

Mum and my stepdad were so supportive and understanding. I think they knew what I had been through and how hard I had tried. Mum always used to say how proud they were of me for always trying to get help, to be well, and how, it was the Mental Health Services who had let me down at the start.

All I wanted to do was to get better and be a better mum for poor Jerry. He was my reason for being here, for living and for wanting to live.

Prior to my admittance to hospital, I had been nominated for a ticket for a Women's Retreat Camp. I had accepted and after discharge, thought it might be a good idea to go. My friend had also booked to come so we were going to travel together. So only a few days after discharge, Mum helped me pack and we headed there by car, took me just over two hours. I was anxious and excited at the same time.

On arrival, a lovely woman in brightly coloured clothes came to greet me, her name was Susan. She smiled and gave me such a hug, reassuring me I would be ok.

We put our tents up, made our beds all cosey and then went to the Opening Ceremony.

Everyone sat on the floor in a circle, I reluctantly joined. Susan welcomed us all, explained about the camp, the activities taking place and some basic rules. It was then over to each individual to check in, if they wished.

I was terrified but when it came to being my turn, I went for it and told everyone how a few days prior to that day, I had been under section under the Mental Health Act, that I was there to have my retreat and maybe help me on my journey to heal.

Little did I realise what an amazing journey I was now about to start! The response to my small introduction was nothing but love, acceptance and comfort.

The weekend was amazing, I tentatively attended some workshops such as;

meditation, art and crafts, love jars etc. All of them and the whole weekend gave me the space, creativity and therapy that I needed at that moment.

I returned home feeling nervous but positive for the future ahead of me. I felt so much love at the retreat and had made some beautiful friends, sisters, we were like a sister family.

They would soon become precious to me in my and my sons' life. I have so much to thank my beautiful sisters for, especially Susan who is now my soul sister and dear friend. They helped me build myself back up, loved me, accepted me, gave me a slap on the buttocks when I needed one, and my bricks. I love them so!

Mum had taken to coming over, we would sometimes go out for coffee and into town doing a bit of clothes shopping.

One of those days in town it was Mental Health Week, Mind had a stand in one of

the shopping centres we went to. Mum encouraged me to go and look.

We went together and I met this lovely woman called Peggy. We started chatting, mum Peggy and myself. Mum told her I had not long come out of hospital; Peggy told us she also had a Mental Health condition. She told me about an art group called In/Out. She gave me a flyer and encouraged me to come.

That Friday, I took a big step and went to the group. The members, including Peggy welcomed me with open arms. We did some painting, each week, they did something different. I became an avid member; I went there for a year or so. I was introduced to so many great things such as singing, crafts, drumming, drama etc. I made some new friends also.

I believe going there was a very important part of my journey, I learnt how to ground myself and activities to help to occupy me, stimulate me and help me to

start feeling better about myself.

I saw Pierre once a month and we chatted about how I was feeling, discussed coping skills and any concerns I have.

He referred me for an Emotional Regulation Group, which I attended, and I learnt so much about BPD and how it affects me, makes me the person I am today.

He later referred me for Psychology with a lady called Katherine. Sessions with her were difficult for me, it was hard to open up, I was scared to, in case it opened up a can of worms and I became unwell again. She was a lovely woman and tried so hard with me. But each meeting, I would feel blocked, I could talk but it was surface talk, I talked about having a gun held at me like I would talk about a day out at the beach. But without feeling or emotion.

 Every session, I became more and more frustrated! I wanted to talk, to talk about my traumas, to release all the hurt and pain that was trapped inside me, but

somehow, I just couldn't.

One evening I sat at home, talking to Jerry about how hard it was. We chatted and I spoke about the Counselling and

Psychotherapy training I had done a few years prior to this. I talked about traumas and good theorists for this. Suddenly, I had a brain fart! Fritz Perl Gestalt Therapy; 'Unfinished Business'! Fritz had designed many ways to release and deal with traumas, with excellent results. Maybe this would help me also.

'Gestalt therapy was designed to help people resolve individual challenges and heal from issues in their pasts that have been preventing them from moving forward with their lives. Many people who get gestalt therapy are suffering from issues related to unhealed trauma, or other mental health issues like anxiety, depression, and post-traumatic stress disorder that have kept them rooted in the past and unable to move forward. In gestalt therapy, a licensed clinical therapist will teach therapy clients how to regain their personal power, through different techniques.' (__How Gestalt Therapy Works to Heal Past Trauma (therapists.com)__ 22/5/23)

My next appointment with Katherine, I mentioned him to her, and we talked about the different techniques Fritz had designed. I asked Katherine if we could do 'The Letter'.

The letter is a technique where you write a letter to the abuser or abusers, telling them how you feel about how they treated you. It is an opportunity to express, let it out, release and get to say what you want to say in safe way. Once the letter is finished, it can be burnt, buried or whatever is safe and best suits the individual.

We decided we would do this. The next session, she gave me a paper and pen. She suggested I start at the beginning. I started to write, I wrote for what seemed like a long time, she then said time was close to the end of the session (it was almost time to end the session?'. I asked her to read it, she suggested I read it.

I did so and felt emotion as I read. Each session, we did this. The letter got longer and longer.

One day, Katherine noted that she felt the letter was ever so kind and polite, she said I can put whatever I wish in the letter, be as polite or impolite as I wish.

That maybe I should really let the abusers, have it?! I took that into account and unformalized my letter and started to really go for it! Swearing, telling one of them straight for what they did to my son, how vile and disgusting they were.

The more I did this, the more I wrote, at the end of each session, reading out what I had read, and starting to open up verbally more and more to Katherine about the traumas I had suffered. The last part of the letter was hard, but I did it. Finalizing, the end, saying goodbye and FUCK OFF. Fuck you! That felt good.

Once the letter was finished, I read it all out to Katherine. I had a cry as did she, she shed a tear for me! That felt strange but comforting that someone felt I was worth crying for. I spoke to her about what I was going to do with the letter.

One of my dear friends Claire had offered to do a full moon fire and releasing ceremony with me. I was planning to read the letter out loud, then put it into the fire. Katherine agreed it was a good idea.

The next full moon, I went to Claires'. We had supper then made the fire. We sat there silently watching the flames build up.

She drummed gently as I read the letter, as I did so, I held my head high and spoke as loud as I needed, shouting the obscenities, and whispering the atrocities I had suffered.

At the end, shouting 'FUCK YOU!'. Shouting that he had not won, I had. That

I was proud of me, he has not beaten me down and I would continue to live my life and be happy. I cried and Claire held me as I did so. It was just what I needed. I had released and felt a huge cloud of relief and freedom. Claire is an amazing friend, more like my sister. I have a lot to thank her for.

Another part of my healing and hopefully to help Jerry also was to say sorry to him.

So, one evening, I asked to speak with him. I explained how I was sorry for, making the wrong choice of men, for not protecting him from the abuse he suffered from his stepfather, for being so unwell during his childhood, for all the traumas he had endured and seen over the years because of me. That I am going to spend the rest of my life trying to make it up to him and show him how strong I am now and make him proud of me.

I explained I do not need his forgiveness and I understand if he cannot forgive me.

I also said anytime in his life he needs to talk to me about our past, whether it is by talking, or shouting, I am there. Always. That I know I made my mistakes as a parent, and I am so sorry also for that.

His response? He was taken aback, saying none of it was my fault, it just happened, and we got through it.

That there was nothing for him to forgive. I told him how much I love him, how proud I am of him for the amazing young man he is, inside and out. We hugged.

If it wasn't for you, I'd be gone by now
....

8.

Borderline Personality Disorder, Who the hell am I?!

Just Like…

Just like a pill…
I have a heavy head,

Just like a drug…
head spinning around and around,

Just like a storm
hyper, hypo, riding the currents,

Just like an ocean…
Up, then down, high then low,

Where do I go?
Ride those waves, Beat that storm, be free!
Blurred lines…

Well, as you know, I have BPD. When I was first diagnosed, I remember going home and looking up about it and how sick I felt inside. It read like I was some kind of an evil monster that overreacts, hurts people, selfish, attention seeking crazy person!

It took years of reading plus then deciding one day to put all the books away and go on a journey to find out about my condition for myself, find out about me, finding out who the hell am I?!! My own personal journey, to find me plus accept and learn to love me.

Why am I like this? Constantly passes through my mind. My mum had had spouts of ill health mentally, maybe it was inherited? My Great grandmother also had poor mental health and spent most of her adult life in a psychiatric unit.

The worst feeling having this condition is the feeling of lack of control, emotions and thoughts run into my head, without any choice. People may think, some even say 'oh, pull yourself together, it is a life choice to be like this, it is all in the mind!' If only that was the case. However, when my BPD kicks off, I do not always have control, although I may have a voice in my head advising me to stop, think a minute before acting, something just takes over me and then I lose control of my mind and what it says, feels, thinks.

It is a terrifying feeling having no control over yourself, your mind.

Hypers, Hypos, Anger, Grey Clouds and Anxiety

There are 5 sides to my BPD.

Hypers

I am rushing, fast, busy, hyper-happy, (edgy also as I know at some point, this feeling can be triggered into anger or

I burn out into rock bottom lowness and suicidal thoughts) Cannot sit still, cannot stop, cannot relax, my heart is pounding so fast I feel like it might explode and burst out of my chest. I talk very very loud, I cannot concentrate or relax, sleeping does not happen.

This goes on for a day, maybe a week or more. It can start by nervousness, anxiety, excitement triggering me, adrenaline rushes but it does not stop, only speeds up more and more. I love the highs, I am happy, oh so so happy! A rush inside of me, pure joy. I do not care about anything; do not see how I am behaving or the dangers it comes with. I say what is in my head, I act out what I want, no repercussions, no fear of anything.

I love the buzz and crave it more and more. I drive fast down a road in the dark with the lights off, I approach men on the streets for sex, I speak to anyone anywhere. I go shopping and spend so much on Jerry and myself. I take Jerry out, spend so much money on him, feeling great about it all. I say exactly what I think, do what I want, I just do not care and have no control at all over this.

Then it burns out or I get triggered. It takes only one little thing to bring me back crashing down to reality. I then suffer anxiety, rages of anger, or deep depression.

Hypos

Lowness, so low, I cannot get out of bed. I have no energy; I have no motivation. I just feel terrible. A huge dark cloud hanging over me, dragging me lower and lower. I don't wash, I don't do anything, I usually just stay in bed where I feel the safest.

When I feel the lowest, I need to sooth or distract, art? Writing? Or self-injury, through using a razor on my wrist.

The pain distracts me from the raw emotional pain I am feeling, it soothes me in a way. Other things I have done is to drink alcohol or smoke weed. None of them really help in the long run, alcohol being a depressant and a few days after my binge, I reach even deeper in the depths of my despair.

Anger

This is what I hate the most! I sadly cannot recall many moments of anger, if I do it is only the aftermath of what I may have said or done. This phase can again happen in whatever phase of my bpd, with the hypers however, I have less control. Lots of things may trigger me, see below the list of symptoms, it may help you understand more.

The feeling I am not enough, that someone will leave me, that I am being put down, hated, not liked, feeling judged, laughed at, shouted at, moaned at, injustice in the world, over protection of those I love, so many things make me see red. If I cause the problem, |I am in control, I self-destruct, that way I did it and I believe it stops me getting hurt. Wanting someone to get me, understand how I am feeling, getting angry when they don't, thinking they don't care!? Wanting that person to feel the hurt I believe they are doing to me. Lashing out verbally, sometimes even physical, but mostly with my mouth, my tongue.

Feeling so many things; irrational, hypersensitive, over-reactive, Delusional, anxious, hyper, swearing, shouting, screaming, lashing out, verbal and physical attacks. I will be in a hyper-aroused state, then I crash, calm down, my body and mind return to calm. Then I remember, I hate myself, punish myself, become overwhelmingly anxious, devasted, embarrassed, hate hate hate overpowers me. Then I may go into anxious or low state.

Grey Cloud

Feeling nothing, empty, devoid of all emotions, nothingness, blank, empty. It is a terrible feeling. Like I am not existing, I am not here. I withdraw. I am nothing at this point.

Anxiety

Becoming anxious but not knowing why. It can appear at any phase of my bpd. If I am in the hyper mode, it is worse as I have no control.

I feel overcome with anxiety, panic, irrational, overthinking, ruminate, delusional, speak to myself, talk myself into hurting myself or not wanting to be on this earth, telling myself I am a 'no good mother, he is better off without you.' I am anxious as I remember how I behaved recently when hyper, I feel overcome with shame and worry what people will think of me. I withdraw into myself, it is safer that way, to self-isolate, then nothing bad will happen. But then, I become very

socially anxious and struggle to go anywhere. I cannot breathe, I hyperventilate, feel sick, suicidal, hurt myself.

- *See below a list of some of the characteristics someone who has BDP may display, plus my own reflection on how it affects me.*

-

1. Constantly Craving Reassurance and Validation

Needing constant attention, reassurance, and validation in order to feel worthy and loved. If I don't get the attention I need, I'll act out or get emotional in order to receive it, which usually is accompanied by word vomit and dissociation.

2. Impulsivity

Being impulsive with my emotions. When I'm upset, I end up making myself look like a mean, angry, unkind person but that's so far from the truth, although in the moment I believe I am horrible for acting that way. Sometimes I'll make a decision and later on, I will realize how irrational I was being and end up in a

situation and have no idea how I ended up there. It's even worse when the situation I create means other people have to help me out when that's the last thing I wanted.

3. Black and White Thinking

Black and white thinking. I don't see the gray in situations. Something is either right or wrong.

4. Over-Sharing

How I can just spill my guts to random people I've just met. I don't know why I do it. They don't need to hear it, it is embarrassing!

5. Paranoia About Relationships

Paranoia and overthinking. If my friends have a neutral expression, I feel like they're mad at me. If they give me a certain look, I feel that they hate me. If they talk to someone else, I assume they want to be their friend, not mine.

Obsession and paranoia over relationships. I am consumed by my feelings whether they're negative or positive — I need constant reassurance from people that they don't hate me or I haven't annoyed them and that they still love me.

Over-texting. When I am anxious and feel like I'm being ignored or abandoned, I will text someone repeatedly, shifting rapidly from anger to apathy to pleading for a response to remorse. I have pushed away so many people, ended relationships and lost friends because of the way I react. When it's happening, I almost can't control it, and it feels logical, but afterwards, I am horrified and ashamed.

6. Fearing Abandonment

I feel like I'm being abandoned. I come up with this whole story in my head about what the said person could be thinking. Then I realize nothing was ever wrong.

The fear of being abandoned. Like I guess it's happened so much to me in my life I always expect everyone to leave and honestly, they usually do, but I feel like it's probably because I assume they are going to.

7. Age Regression

Age regression. I find myself always wanting to relate to people on a swayed ground of power. More often than not, this is with me being the dependent party, and I become very childlike (and then get upset when people infantilize me). I am often mistaken for being much much younger than I actually am.

8. Being Unable to Take Rejection or Criticism

The worst one is probably my inability to take rejection. Like, at all. I overreact in response to it, and it just makes things worse for everyone involved. Half the time, I wasn't even being rejected, I just thought I was.

9. Dissociation

Completely dissociating over minor issues, losing control and hurting myself... What really gets to me about this is that I genuinely love my life but even that won't stop me from hurting myself in those moments. I dissociate and have gaps in my memory. People don't understand how I can go from having no memory of my life for certain months and/or years but then turn around and remember other things in great detail.

10. Pushing People Away

Being terrified of being alone, then pushing away everyone who cares about me because I feel unworthy of their friendship. Pushing people away when I feel they may reject me.

11. Being "Clingy"

My two mind sets. I am either pushing people away without even realizing it to make sure they don't abandon me, or I'm beyond clingy to make sure they don't abandon me. I absolutely hate it. I am either too much or nothing at all. I feel everything at once.

I'm thankful I have loved ones who understand and stays with me through it all when even I want to leave myself. I hate it. — It makes me really clingy and insecure. I always claw at people, and I drive them away by being too emotional.

12. Being Unable to Control Emotional "Outbursts"

Outbursts of emotions. I can't always handle them because they simply take over. Seeing myself afterwards is the most embarrassing thing ever, like I have made a total fool of myself, looking into others faces being judged for

some kind of incapability.

My first response to any negative emotion is to cry, I can't control it. I've burst into tears on the bus, in the middle of busy streets and at work. Then when people want to know why I'm crying and try to help me, it makes me cry more.

13. Overthinking

Overthinking and adding things up to prove a loved one is lying in my head and end up crying all day because I have no idea if my intuition is correct because I can't trust my own thoughts.

14. Explosive Anger

My sudden explosive anger over very minute things. I say stuff that's harmful and so cruel without even realizing it. Once the anger subsides a few moments later, I am burdened with such guilt and shame over what I just did.

Then I hear about what exactly I said and it's downright heart-breaking. Now that I finally know what the cause is and the symptoms, I can properly take actions to manage it. It's nice knowing the enemy you're going to war with.

15. Feeling Like You're "Too Much"

I don't know [if] I'm being 'too much' until it's too late, and then I'm embarrassed that I can't seem to control it. Too emotional, too sad, too this or that.

16. Being Consumed By Sex or Experiencing Sexual Repulsion

My constant switching between hypersexuality and sexual repulsion. I get into a mindset of dangerous sexual promiscuity, then suddenly find myself disgusted by anyone and everyone and never wanting to be touched ever again.

Every time I thought I was doing it for myself to make that person like me or love me more, and then it turns out they end up leaving

because I'm too complicated or they don't understand what BPD is. Or because I was just for sex, had no respect for me as a person, woman, why would they when I couldn't even respect myself?!

17. Having "Inappropriate" Reactions

My completely inappropriate reactions to things. Smiling when people talk about negative things, getting extremely angry over the seemingly smallest problem, feeling like my chest is literally exploding when I get excited. Everything is amplified up to 11. Most people around me don't seem to understand this. Saying inappropriate things when nervous, excitable or manic. I struggle to filter my thoughts when I'm calm, but it's so much worse when I'm uncomfortable. This is always followed by feelings of intense guilt and self-hatred. Then I tend to go into my shell after and avoid people who were about when it happened.

Anxiety going out anywhere in case I get like it again. Social anxiety taking over me.

18. Feeling "Irrational"

How quickly I can change from the most rational person to completely irrational and not understanding that I'm being irrational until the time has passed. Paranoia about friends and family not really loving me, that they will leave, I am 'too much' for everyone. No self-worth at all.

19. "Flaking" on Plans

I cancel plans constantly because of the extreme fear that I'm just a bother, having no energy after a manic episode or just being too anxious. Worst of all I will cancel and make an excuse rather than saying I am not feeling well. Why? Shame? Embarrassment?

20 Being "Obsessive"

Being obsessive. about things, items, thoughts paranoias etc. If I had something in my head, thought something, it was hard to get rid of it.

I can obsess over things sometimes for months, and that takes a toll on me. But the other people having to hear my endless complaining.

21. Being the Centre of Conversations

I tend to overwhelm conversations without meaning to. I constantly 'one up' others, which I know is annoying but really conversation is hard for me and I'm just trying to participate so I don't look antisocial or plain rude. Being socially awkward.

22. Manipulating Others Without Meaning To

Being manipulative but not intending to.

23. Not Knowing Who You Are

The most embarrassing thing I faced when I was first diagnosed was not really having a full grasp of who I really was, not knowing what was the condition and what was me? I did not know who I or what I was!

What helps me now?

Every day is different, one day one thing will work, another it won't. It is because of that, I have a list of things that I use/ try. See below :

- My beliefs
- Pagan gatherings
- Spell Casting
- Meditation
- Manifesting positivity
- Exercise
- Writing my journal
- Art
- Polly my dog cuddles
- Reaching out
- Mind Maps
- Problem solving
- Music
- Drumming
- Seeing a friend

- Calling and seeing my GP
- Mental Health Link Worker
- Calling Samaritans
- Having a bath
- Going to bed
- PJ day
- Camping
- Holidays
- Reading a good book
- Planning my diary so I have things to look forward to
- Etc every day I am researching and trying out new things

9.
Hold on …………and there is more?!

Wandering

Wandering, meandering without purpose

Seeking, reaching out, needing that sign

Needing, needing to feel, to get that release

Reaching, reaching out, to feel you there

Feeling, feeling the need to see you

Thinking, thinking of the happy times and memories

Remembering, remembering the love I have for you

Looking, searching for you, your spirit, come to me

Forgive me, forgive me for saying good bye

Begging, please show me, be there, say good bye

Farewell, my love, go to the light, walk free

Good bye, my love…Sssshhhhhh!

Well, you would be hoping now I am near to the end of this book, that the worst is over!?

To reflect on my life has been a hard and emotional one, some things I haven't even started to grieve over, let alone release as yet.

So, after all the shit happened and I was living a pretty happy life, I met the love of my life, I will call him Jazzy G. We met on a dating site, shared a few messages, swapped numbers and after a while of chatting, he asked me on a date.

He lived in Surrey, just past Wimbledon. I at the time was working for a charity and monthly would travel to its headquarters in London for meetings. It made sense to meet when I was next to be in London.

I am smiling as I write this, remembering our special times together, how lovely it feels!

We met outside a coffee shop and went for a drink at this wacky, special looking pub in Battersea. It had a lovely garden with chairs and snuggle blankets. I

I was so nervous, but Jazzy G had a jovial manner which soon made me feel at ease. We ended up going back to my hotel and chatted and kissed all night till the early hours.

We spent some amazing times together over the next few years. He made me feel special and loved in a way no man has ever done. Some examples of them are; staying in a Penthouse Suite on the top floor of flush apartments in Brixton with a garden at the top, a beautiful terrace to see all of London, a spectacular sight, going on a speed boat over the River Thames at full speed with James Bond music playing. Camping, going to festivals together and so on.

Just being together was enough. He made love to me so gently and with so much passion as if I was the most beautiful and precious woman on this earth. I felt so loved.

The only problem which ended up finishing us was his drug addiction, weed and coke. He had started at a very young age and all his efforts to stop failed with him not being able to resist the way it made him feel. It caused Drug Induced Psychosis, he believed in many Conspiracies, but it ended up with such paranoia, it took over his life. I tried to help him, encourage him but after a few years, I saw this was how it was going to be and I could not cope with the pain of seeing him killing himself any longer.

He died roughly a year after I ended it, I still love him and will always love him. I am just so grateful a month before he died, we had a lovely chat on the phone, I told him how I will always love him. We had our last special moment and I hope he believed what I said that day. I am eternally grateful to him for helping me to love myself for who I am and for all the love and laughter he brought and gave to me.

I miss him, but sometimes I can feel his presence is with me. I will always have guilt for him passing, that maybe my walking away made him worse; it is something I will never know and will carry to my grave; whether or not it was my fault. But with that thought, I know I, at the time, did what was right for me. It didn't stop me loving him or missing him, it still doesn't.

Thank you, Jazzy G, hope you're having fun up there with your bro!

I Love you. Namaste.
Sssshhhhhh..........(his term of endearment he used to use)

So now to my mum. Mum was mum, hard to explain. She loved me and Jerry so much. Her life was devoted to her family.

She was married to Jock, who was my stepdad, but often took the role of my father, which I loved and appreciated.

They lived in a town house an hour or

so away from us. They spent their summers camping with their little caravan in places around the UK, such as Scotland, Yorkshire, The New Forest, Cornwall, Thetford etc.

They had taken a large role in helping me bring up Jerry, having him in some school holidays if I was working, taking him and myself sometimes camping with them. Jerry and I were both very close with them.

Every Christmas, we would take it in turns, one year at mine and one year at theirs. They were a huge presence in both our lives.

Mum had cancer 3 times, the first time in her throat, well her neck and it was cut out and all was well. Several years later, she got breast cancer. She had a partial mastectomy and chemotherapy. A year or so later, she got the all clear. It knocked her emotionally and took its toll on her I feel.

Several years later, during COVID, mum started to feel unwell. She had a chest infection, but it didn't go.

It got worse and she was then finding it hard to breathe. I remember the call when Jock told me mum was in ambulance on the way to hospital, having issues breathing. The worst thing was normally a daughter would get in the car and be by her bedside holding her hand, however, due to COVID restrictions, I was unable to be with her.

She had tests and two days later, she called me, crying, the Consultant had come and told her the Cancer was back and it had gone to her lungs. My poor mum was told this news when she was in a side room, alone without any family by her side!

The family wanted to show her how much she is loved so my sister and I asked people to send us messages for her, we printed them off, as well as pictures the great grandchildren did for her and I did some art. I collated this into a large scrap book for her. I planned to visit the hospital, drop this off to her ward. I also decided to reach out to her from my car outside her ward. I planned to park outside, play 'I'll be there' by the Jackson Five loudly with all doors open, call mum, and ask her to come to the window, then sign the words in Makaton to her.

Meanwhile! They drained her lungs of the fluid that had gathered and then mum discharged herself, saying it was making her feel worse mentally being in there.

So, instead of driving to the hospital, I drove to mum's and parked outside, I beeped my horn and waited for them both to come to the door. Jock opened the door and he called Mum. Mum also came and stood at the door, looking shocked to see me there.

She stood and leant against Jock as I pr

oceeded to play the song full blast and sign it to her. I had already dropped the scrap book outside her house in a box with lots of gifts from us all.

Mum smiled and smiled, then burst into tears. I sent her a hug from across the road, crying also as I got into my car and made the journey back home, in pieces seeing my mum but not being able to hug her or kiss her.

She fought the cancer with a vengeance. She said she was not ready to die yet and accepted all treatments offered to her. A few months later, Jock started to feel unwell, and he was diagnosed with bowel cancer, inoperable. He refused treatment apart from painkillers, preferring instead to concentrate on loving and caring for mum.

Each week, I visited mum a few times, when I could. One of those days every week, when she was able, I took her out, for a coffee, for lunch, shopping, to

the seaside, wherever she wanted to go, I now treasure those beautiful memories.

One Sunday, I had a call from my cousin Andy. She was crying. My Uncle (Mum's brother) had been found dead in his flat. We were all devastated, and I had the awful job of breaking the news to mum.

COVID restrictions were over at this point, so I was able to visit her and hold her hand as I broke the dreadful news to her. 'Noooo she shouted, not MY Tony!' she sobbed as I held her. Mum lost her fight to cancer three days after this.

She had not wanted to go into hospital but was in so much pain, her GP called an ambulance and mum agreed to go to hospital. It was then they told us mum was dying and now going to receive 'end of life care'.

My sister, niece, Jerry, Jock, and I took it in turns to sit with her. My sister brought her headphones and played mum's favorite music in her ears.

My niece brought some massage lotion and massaged mum's hands and arms. Rose lotion it was, mum smelt lovely.

I brought crystals and placed them in each of her hands. I played music mum loved and also a song my dear friend Susan had sung; a lullaby she recorded it especially for my mum.

Mum waited for Jerry to finish his work shift and I went with him to visit her. He sat beside her, holding her hands, stroking her cheeks, speaking gently to her, telling her how much he loves her. Mum passed quietly and peacefully just 2 hours after Jerry and I left the hospital.

Roughly 2 months later, Jock passed away peacefully at home, after having spent a nice day with Jerry and I, and the evening with my sister and niece. That evening, my sister was trying to sleep in the chair next to him whilst he was sleeping intermittently on his sofa. During

the night, he awoke, gasping, my sister sat in front of him, he held on to her hands, looking at her, she mouthed quietly 'I love you' as he then took his last breath.

I was so lucky having 2 dads, my blood dad in Africa, who I love and dearly miss and Jock. Jock did a lot for Jerry and me. A huge loss for us both.

In over a year, we lost so many loved ones. It is so hard to come to terms with it all. But I plodded on as I do nowadays.

Work was great, working at a Local University as a Residential Life Advisor. But following the bereavements, came a tough time at work; losing two students, finding one of them dead who had ended her life. I coped well and supported students affected. We all battled on and I felt ok.

2 weeks later, I was due to be on a late shift. In the morning, I went to the local gym and had a Personal Training

Session. I loved it. I then drove to work and settled into my job for the afternoon.

After about an hour of being there, I started to feel a pins and needle type feeling in my neck, which then felt like heart burn. I took gentle breaths thinking it will pass. After five minutes, I felt pains like a cramp feeling in my chest, close to my heart. I again gently breathed thinking it may be a stitch from doing gym that morning. 30 mins later, it was still there, and I knew I was in trouble.

I radioed Security and asked for them to come to the office as I thought I was having a heart attack. An hour later I was in A&E with a suspected heart attack. Four weeks later, I am discharged after having surgery to fit a Pacemaker, diagnosis Cardiomyopathy and two other things I can't remember. I am now convalescing, having to take things slow. At one point, my heart was failing and at 15% function, a very scary time for me.

During my stay in hospital, I reached out for love and support, because I was scared and needed my loved ones. One person told me I was 'emotionally blackmailing people' and proceeded to get funny with me. Some family members never visited, which hurt me a lot.

At times like this, you find out who counts. Jerry has been amazing as I expected, and also my sister and niece and two dear friends. I am so lucky. I have had to make some difficult decisions though, one being to walk away from stress and drama, that is not being taken well by some people but right now, I have to think of me, those that know me understand.

Whilst in hospital, I did not have many visitors, sometimes, I would cry as felt and and like I was not important to some people. Across the bay was Tabitha. Her family and her took to supporting me during my stay in hospital, as well as

some other lovely families.

Tabitha and I became great friends, both had a little giggle and were like school kids, misbehaving on the ward.

Sadly, she died a month after I was discharged, a huge loss for me. I was so excited having my new friend and we both had many plans to have some fun together in our lives.

Since discharge, I have had to start life again, differently. I will permanently have heart failure and the pacemaker is working 24/7 to keep me alive. That is hard to come to terms with. But I am trying to, I am grateful I am alive and believe it was not my time, that I have a second chance

at life.

My motto is many, to live every day as if it is my last and grasp every opportunity with both hands.

Right now, I am working on rehabilitation. Getting as strong as I can be. Listening to my body. Being self-aware both physically and mentally.

That means minimal stress and having to walk from people causing me such. Working on my physical and mental health, using mindfulness and my spirituality to help me.

It is going to be a difficult journey but, I know I can do it.

10.

Here I am! My Hopes and Dreams Everyday...

May everyday...the sun shine
the flowers blossom
and the colours just brighten your day!

May everyday...Mother Earth shine
shine down on you
fill your heart with love and spring in your step!
    Blessed Be x

Ok, so this is going to a great chapter to write as my goodness, there have been some bloody hard ones!

Firstly, where am I now?

Well, I am in my little council house in a quaint village, living with my son who is now 29yrs old, our 20yr old dog Polly and a funny little diva Sphinx called Meena. It is a peaceful place and a nice, quiet life.

Jerry has qualified in his job, he is an Emergency services worker, recently having been promoted. He also has a thriving business buying and selling antiques and oddities. I am so proud of him, we are close, more like best friends. I have so much I am grateful to gi for, most importantly for coming into my life and being my angel.

I also have three beautiful stepdaughters whom I love dearly. I also have a scrumbdiddlyumptious step-granddaughter, who I adore, she is a cheeky little cherub, with big brown eyes and jet black curly hair. Chunky little legs, beautiful skin, all these attritbutes akin to that of a precious china doll. I adore her!

I work at a local University; I work there as a Residential Life Advisor within the Student Support Team.

In my spare time, I like to draw, paint, colour, write, play and listen to music, get outside and camping in the summer at different festivals. I consider myself a Solitary Witch, I believe in Mother Earth and all the other Goddesses and Deities there are. I manifest and can make spells, as well as am now a qualified Reiki Practitioner.

I offer readings for people and am now and am planning to set up my own Life Coaching and Mindfulness Business, which will include readings, Reiki, self-help groups, workshops etc.

I am happy, I have accepted my Mental Health Condition and accepted me, for who I am, and I kind of like who I am, in fact I love some of it!

I have accepted I can see into the other realms, I see, smell, hear and feel spirits that have passed over. I used to think it was me seeing things due to my Mental Illness, but it is not. It is a great gift and I am learning to embrace my skills and abilities.

I am now recovered as best I can be from my heart attack and the pacemaker being fitted. Coming to terms with it all is difficult but I realise is a part of my life journey. I will recover and am not ready to leave this world yet, heck no!

Life is way too short, dwelling on what happened or what could have been, quitefrankly is a waste of my time. Now? Me? Future? To live every day as if it was my last, not take anything or anybody for granted. To be a little selfish and think more about me and what I want, need.

One last thing; Be you! It does not matter what people think, be the beautiful person you want to and are meant to be!

I am finally embracing me! I have just got back from a beautiful Lammas Gathering, a weekend in Derbyshire with like minded people. I was completely and unforgivingly myself. I had dreadlocks fitted and I now dress as I want to and am being who I want to be. Yes it is a bit weird and bright and wonderful, but it is me and who I am. And I am proud of that!

Watch this space …….or not!

Why did I name this book 'how to grow sunflowers'?

Mum and I enjoyed our special days out together. We would often go for drives in the countryside, then stop for a coffee and some cake in a nice coffee shop. Mum and I enjoyed looking at the scenery and she would pick out any flowers she saw. She particularly liked sunflowers and poppies.

I feel growing a sunflower is a process, it takes time to reach its full potential and flower into a beautiful thing, similar to life. Plus a sunflower to me signifies peace, beauty and happiness, which this book is all about, my quest to self-acceptance, self-love and happiness and I believe I have blossomed into a very beautiful, special flower. Plus I just love sunflowers! ☐

Blessed be to you and thanks for reading my mumblings xxx

My Dreams, My Goals, My Bucket List!

- Jamaica – did it with my boy. Sooo going to do it again with him!

- Write my book and get it published – oh yes it will happen!

- Learn more and study Paganism and further develop my skills and abilities in it

- Study for Teacher In Mindfulness Qualification

- Set up my own business in Mindfulness & healing – on its way baby!

- Continue with my arts and crafts, and sell my work on Etsy
- Do a painting course
- Buy my own home
- Build a therapy room and music room in my garden
- Continue to watch and be proud of my son and his achievements in life, as well as maybe hiccups along the way
- Get to live to be a Grandmother!
- Egypt, Pyramids
- Morocco
- Go on a cruise
- Waterfall experience
- Forest experience
- Have a hot tub and bar in my garden
- Learn how not to be scared swimming out of my depth

- Try wild water swimming
- Lose weight
- Get fitter, go back to the gym and enjoy it!
- Stretch limo to see a show in London and stay in a swanky hotel
- Get my nipples pierced again
- Tattoo finish on back, plus sleeve to be completed
- Get a pet goat and a pig
- Continue to be happy in myself
- Get my son some kind of award for how amazing he has been to me
- When I retire ; buy a long boat and a piece of land. Land to have a yurt, garden and hot tub. Also have a camper van. Travel Europe, see beautiful sights, write another book! Chill, be happy, relax and breathe
  ………………………………………
  ………………..!!

I am me and I like me! I am ok! I will be ok!

Printed in Great Britain
by Amazon